AIRLINER 3

BOEING 707

P.R.SMITH

Copyright © Paul R. Smith 1991

First published in the UK in 1991 by
Airlife Publishing Ltd.

British Library Cataloguing in Publication Data
Smith, P. R. (Paul Raymond), *1966 –*
   Boeing 707.
   1. Aeroplanes
   I. Title
   629.13334

   ISBN 1-85310-087-0

Printed in Singapore by Kyodo Printing Co (S'pore) Pte Ltd

Airlife Publishing Ltd.

101 Longden Road, Shrewsbury, SY3 9EB, England.

Introduction

It was a $16 million gamble that was waiting for flight on the threshold of the runway in Renton, Washington, on July 15 1954. The Boeing design model 367-80, known to the public as the prototype Boeing 707, sat awaiting, be it somewhat restlessly, for her pilot, A. M. 'Tex' Johnston, to release the brake. Her four 10,000 pound thrust engines were straining against an invisible harness for the freedom that only speed and altitude could provide. When she finally broke free, little did her owners know that this was the start of the most successful family of commercial jet aircraft ever to be built.

To many, the 'Dash Eighty' was just another jet aircraft. After all, the six-engine Boeing B-47 Stratojet, had been flying since 1947. However, to the tenacious builders of the -80, this aircraft was the finale to almost ten years of dreams, blood, sweat and tears. It was Boeing that had stuck out its neck in the belief that a requirement for a commercial jet transport was needed. Indeed it was to the tune of $16 million that was being gambled, in the face of heavy odds, since the two markets, the airlines, and the military, were both passive. A new jet transport with a predicted price tag running close to $16 million per unit could not be justified. On September 1 1954, the United States Air Force contracted with Boeing for 29 tanker versions of the Dash Eighty which were given the Boeing model number 717. Nevertheless, sales of the commercial transport version, the 707, were not immediately forthcoming and Boeing executives began to ponder the possibility that they might just have a white elephant on their hands. They were also worried about Douglas's new DC-8, a jet powered transport, equipped like the 707, with Pratt and Whitney JT3's. There now followed what became known as the 'Boeing-Douglas jet transport sales race'. Sales began to break for Boeing, Juan Trippe, President of Pan American World Airways, became interested in the 707. Always in the vanguard, he persuaded Pan Am to invest $296 million in the jet. The order was placed on October 13 1955, and was the largest order for commercial transport ever placed. Following Pan Am's purchase, United Air Lines announced it would buy 30 DC-8s, and Bill Allen, President of Boeing, told his staff to work harder. They did, and on November 8 1955, American Airlines bought 30 707s.

At the same time Pan Am purchased the 707s, however, the company also placed an order with Douglas for 25 DC-8s. Boeing went into production at once, and delivered the first 707-120, the production model, to Pan Am on August 15 1958, three months ahead of schedule.

There were several variations to the basic 367-80 model, and details of some of them are as follows: **707-120.** The first production model of the 707 class was a close approximation of the -80. Called the Stratoliner after its namesake, the four-engined, tail-dragging, propeller-driven transport of the pre-war years, the -120 emerged from the prototype with basically similar lines. It was, however, larger in size, had more powerful engines, and a slightly higher gross weight than its older sister-ship. **707-138.** A special version of the -120 was built exclusively for Quantas Empire Airway Ltd of Australia. The custom ship, model 707-138, was essentially the same as the -120, but had a 10-foot shorter fuselage. **707-220.** Braniff International Airways wasn't quite satisfied with the performance of the -120, so it signed a purchase order for the specially-built -220s. Other than having more powerful turbojet engines, the -220 is identical to the -120. **VC-137A.** The purchase of three special -120s by the Air Force was authorised by Congress in 1958. From the outside the three VC-137As were identical to all pre-existing 707-120s with the exception of the easily-recognisable paint schemes. Intended to carry the President of the United States and other high government officials, the three distinguished aircraft bare the awesome inscription 'United States of America' across their fuselage. Manufactured with custom-design interiors and carrying the most modern electronic equipment available, the three VC-137As have extraordinary communication capabilities. Hot lines, coded frequencies, and a host of other secret 'black boxes' make it possible, in time of emergency, for airborne officials to contribute to the command and control of America's defense forces. The ship which carries the President is identified by the radio call 'Air Force One'. This could be any one of the 'VC' aircraft or any other aircraft transporting the nation's highest official. A portable presidential seal is affixed to 'Air Force One' whenever the President is on board.

707-320. Largest members of the 707 tribe are the Intercontinentals, the generic name given to the -320s. Again, the -320 has similar lines to its smaller counterpart, the -120. the mightier Intercontinental boasts an almost 3.6m (12ft) increase in wingspan, a 2.4m (8ft) longer fuselage, and an increase in gross weight of 27,215kg (68,000lb). Designed for carrying up to 189 passengers, the long range 707 served the lengthiest routes in the world.

KC-135A. A logical follow-on to the prototype 707 was the military Stratotanker, designed as a mid-air refuelling platform for the Strategic Air Command's growing jet bomber fleet. The KC-135A is similar in design and overall size to the -80, but has only a single large cargo door instead of two. The excess fuel is carried in fuel tanks located in the lower lobe of the double-deck fuselage, allowing an unobstructed upper deck for cargo and personnel transport. It is interesting to note that, popular to other ideas, the factory designation for the KC-135A is the 'Boeing 717'. **C-135A.** The Stratolifter was ordered by the Military Air Transport Command for re-equipping its logistic transport fleet. Except for a larger 707-type vertical tail and the elimination of the refuelling capability, the C-135A Stratolifter is almost identical to its SAC counterpart.

Despite the fact that the majority of 707s have been retired from service and have now gone to the 'great white airport in the sky' it should be pointed out that a few still remain in service today. Therefore, next time you are at your local airport, especially in North and South America, and Africa, keep a look out for that familiar design. You wouldn't be wrong in thinking that you had seen a Boeing 707.

TABLE OF COMPARISONS

	367-80 (PROTOTYPE)	707-320
Max. accommodation:	Prototype	189
Wing span:	39.62 m (130 ft)	43.41 m (142 ft 5 in)
Length:	38.4 m (126 ft)	46.61 m (152 ft 11 in)
Max. t/o weight:	72,574 kg (160,000 lb)	143,334 kg (316,000 lb)
Max. cruis. speed:	966 km/h (600 mph)	966 km/h (600 mph)
Max. range:	3218 km (2000 miles)	6759 km (4200 miles)
Service ceiling:	12,802 m (42,000 ft)	12,497 m (41,000 ft)

	707-120	707-320C
Max. accommodation:	181 passengers	219 passengers or 96,800 lb of cargo
Wing span:	39.88 m (130 ft 10 in)	44.42 m (145 ft 9 in)
Length:	44.22 m (145 ft 1 in)	46.61 m (152 ft 11 in)
Max. t/o weight:	112,490 kg (248,000 lb)	152,406 kg (336,000 lb)
Max. cruis. speed:	966 km/h (600 mph)	966 km/h (600 mph)
Max. range:	4828 km (3000 miles)	6437 km (4000 miles)
Service ceiling:	12,497 m (41,000 ft)	12,497 m (41,000 ft)

	707-220
Max. accommodation:	167 passengers
Wing span:	39.88 m (130 ft 10 in)
Length:	41.68 m (136 ft 9 in)
Max. t/o weight:	104,326 kg (230,000 lb)
Max. cruis. speed:	946 km/h (600 mph)
Max. range:	4828 km (3000 miles)
Service ceiling:	12,497 m (41,000 ft)

AER LINGUS (EI/EIN)

Ireland

Aer Lingus. the national airline of the Republic of Ireland, was originally formed on May 22 1936, by the Irish Government. It was given technical assistance by Blackpool and West Coast Air Services, to operate a single de Havilland Dragon to Bristol. The Irish carrier was eventually merged with the international Aerlinte Eirann, which was itself formed in 1947. The two companies were fully integrated, and the resulting Aer Lingus now maintains an impressive scheduled passenger and freight route network that links the Republic with cities in the United Kingdom, Europe and the United States. The Irish flag carrier maintains a fleet of Boeing 737 aircraft, and became one of the world's first airlines to operate all current models of the type (ie -300, -400 and -500), as well as the older -200 series. Other types maintained include the Boeing 747, 767, Fokker 50 and Saab 340B. The latter two examples form part of

the Aer Lingus Commuter service, maintained by the company, for domestic services, and certain routes to the UK. The BAe 1-11s and Shorts 360s which until 1990, formed part of the main fleet, have now been sold. The company livery, designed by King and Wetherell, reflects a bold national identity through the use of predominantly green colouring and Irish Shamrock logos. The fuselage displays a distinctive bright green roof and dark green windowline, separated by a band of bright blue, with the lower section in white and the belly in grey. A simple Shamrock is worn on the fin in white, and repeated alongside the 'Aer Lingus' fuselage lettering in bright green. The Boeing 707 is no longer operated by the airline, but, the first example in the current livery, then new, went into service during the first week of December 1974. The carrier maintains the ICAO call sign 'SHAMROCK'.

AEROLINEAS ARGENTINAS (AR/ARG)

Argentina

Aerolineas Argentinas was founded as a state corporation in May 1949, by the Ministry of Transport to take over the operations of Fama, Alfa, Aeroposta and Zarda. These companies finally ceased operation in December of that year, and were subsequently merged to form the Argentinian flag carrier. Today the airline operates an extensive network of scheduled passenger and cargo routes to points in North, South and Central America, New Zealand, the Far East, South Africa and Europe. International services radiate from Buenos Aires to Cape Town, Madrid, Rome, Zurich, Frankfurt, Paris (CDG), Los Angeles, Miami, New York (JFK), Montreal, Rio de Janeiro, Sao Paulo, Asuncion, Montevideo, La Paz, Caracas, Lima, Santiago, Guayaquil, Bogota, Port Alegre, Mexico City, Hong Kong and Auckland. It should be noted that on January 21 1990, Aerolineas Argentinas re-introduced flights to London (LHR), the first time it had done so since the Falklands conflict, and the cessation of all services between the UK and Argentina. The aircraft operating that first scheduled service, flight number AR 166, was Boeing 747-287B, LV-OOZ. A fleet of Boeing 707, 727, 737, 747 and Fokker F-28 types is maintained. All aircraft utilised by Aerolineas Argentinas wear an identical livery, which features twin cheatlines in medium and dark blue, extending from the nose, widening along the fuselage, and terminating on the fin, where each is topped by a similarly coloured 'A' initial. Dark blue 'Aerolineas Argentinas' titles are carried on the forward fuselage, as is the traditional bird logo. Seen here, Boeing 707-387C, LV-JGR at Basel Airport, on September 8 1985. The carrier's ICAO call sign is 'ARGENTINA'. *(W. Kathe)*

AFRICAN INTERNATIONAL
AIRWAYS (QA/AEK)

Kenya

African International Airways is a Nairobi-based charter carrier, which is a subsidiary of Equator Airlines. The company was originally known as African Express Airways — Kenya, but changed its name in 1985. Today is offers worldwide ad-hoc and contract passenger services from its base at Nairobi's Embakasi Airport. The first Boeing 707-351C employed by the company was one leased from ZAS Airlines of Egypt. Although still with the airline, the aircraft initially sported a livery which was very similar to Jamahirya Air Transport, a previous operator of this particular Boeing 707. Little in the way of alteration was made to the distinctive green and white scheme of the Libyan airline, since the green, as well as being the Middle Eastern country's national colours, also appears on the Kenyan flag, along with black and red stripes. Black and red also coloured the simple 'AE' motif which occupied the white tail disk, vacated by the Jamahiryan's 'Antelope head' symbol, whilst full-length 'African Express Airways' titling, in black, was displayed on the cabin roof, preceded by a facsimile of the Kenyan flag.

Today, the livery has not changed a great deal. However, gone is the window-level green cheatline, and in its place is a blue stripe below the windows. Out is the white disk, in its place being the 'AE' symbol on its own, still coloured in red and black, against a white background. 'African International Airways' titling is displayed on the forward fuselage, now that the company name has changed. Seen here at Stansted Airport is 5Y-AXA, Boeing 707-338C, during September 1986. Although no longer with the airline, the aircraft is depicted wearing the current livery, although the change of name had not, at that stage, come into effect. It had made its maiden voyage on November 20 1967, and was delivered to Qantas Airways, its first operator, in December of that year. The aircraft subsequently saw service worldwide, before being leased by the then African Express Airways in April 1986. Following the 707's return to ZAS Airlines of Egypt, it was sold in the USA, where it is still operating. *(Author's Collection)*

AIR FRANCE (AF/AFR)   France

Air France was founded on August 30 1933, when Societe Centrale pour l'Exploitation De Lignes Aeriennes (formed shortly before, on May 19, by the merger of Air Orient, Air Union, Compagnie Internationale de Navigation Aerienne, and Societe Generale de Transport Aerienne) purchased the assets of Compagnie Generale Aeropostale. After the Second World War air transport was nationalised and Societe Nationale Air France was set up on January 1 1946, followed by Compagnie Nationale Air France on June 16 1948, when the airline was incorporated by Act of Parliament. The flag carrier became one of the launch customers for the Airbus A340 in January 1987. It lost its monopoly on flights to the French overseas territories in 1986, when Minerve and Point Air were licensed to operate charter flights alongside Air France's services. The state currently has a 99.38 per cent holding in the carrier. A comprehensive network covers an intricate pattern of medium haul routes throughout Europe, North Africa and the Middle East, and a long haul network extends to North and South America, the Caribbean Islands, Africa, Madagascar, and the Indian Ocean, China, Japan and other points in the Far East. Air France also operates the French Postal Administration night mail services. Some European routes are maintained by Transport Aerien Transregional (formerly known as Touraine Air Transport), as well as by Air Littoral, Britair, Europe Air, Air Limousin and Brymon Airways. The carrier is the only airline to operate to all of the United Kingdom's main, and regional, airports from its base at Paris (CDG). Air France operates a fleet of Concorde, Boeing 727, 737, 747, Airbus A300, A310, A320, Fokker F-27 and Transall types. When the present colour scheme was adopted in 1975, it was widely acclaimed as something totally new in airline livery design. A white overall fuselage finish is highlighted by blue 'Air France' fuselage titles and a very small horse logo, the famous 'Cleval Vapeur', in blue and red. The tail fin displays the major splash of colour in the form of blue and red stripes in varying widths. Pure-freight aircraft can be identified by additional 'Cargo' titling alongside the company name. This is, however, separated from the main lettering by a 'Flying Pelican'. Depicted here, whilst on approach to London's Heathrow Airport, is Boeing 707-328, 'Chateau de Maintenon', F-BHSL. The aircraft had operated a flight from Paris (CDG), on November 2, 1973, and is seen sporting the carrier's previous livery. The airline's ICAO call sign is 'AIR FRANCE'. *(B. J. Eagles)*

AIR GUINEE (GI/GIB)

Guinea

The West African Republic of Guinea's national airline was established in October 1960, with a base at Conakry, following the signing of an agreement with the Soviet Union in March of that year, for the supply of aircraft and technical assistance. Operations started towards the end of that year with Ilyushin Il-14s, over two domestic routes from Conakry to Boke and Kankan. Today it employs a mixed fleet of Soviet and western-built aircraft to serve an extensive domestic passenger network, as well as flying regional scheduled services to points in neighbouring countries, including Dakar (Senegal), Freetown (Sierra Leone), Monrovia (Liberia), Abidjan (Ivory Coast), Lagos (Nigeria) and Bissau (Guinea Bissau). Ad-hoc charters are also flown regionally and to Europe. In 1985 it was planned by the airline to operate scheduled services to Europe, using Airbus A300 equipment, although nothing concrete ever came of this idea. Both Paris (CDG) and Brussels were the likliest of destinations. Although a destination in the UK was considered. Although the Boeing 707 depicted here is no longer operated by Air Guinea, a single Boeing 737 type is maintained, together with an Ilyushin Il-18 for VIP and ad-hoc charters, several Antonov An-24s, a Dash-7, Twin Otter and Yak-40 for domestic services. Centrepiece of the company's stylish visual image is the tail fin, which is green with a large yellow map of Africa, superimposed on a number of horizontal stripes. It should be noted that a highlight of a small red area of the map pinpoints the location of the Guinea Republic. The national red, yellow and green colour the cheatlines, which extend along the entire fuselage length, just below the windows, and by the forward passenger door appears the Guinean flag and red 'Air Guinee' company titling.

AIR INDIA (AI/AIC)

India

Air India was formed to succeed Tata Airlines (founded in 1932), which began air mail flights over a Karachi-Ahmedabad-Bombay-Bellary-Madras route on October 15, 1932. Privately-controlled Tata became publicly-owned Air India in July 1946. On June 8 1948 an Air India International division opened, a Bombay-Basra-Cairo-Geneva-London (LHR) line, using a fleet of three Lockheed Super Constellations. When private Indian airlines were nationalised in 1953, the government created one domestic and one international flag carrier — Air India International became the international operator, while Air India was merged with seven other carriers to form Indian Airlines Corporation. Besides the initial London service, other important Air India inaugurals included service to Tokyo, in May 1955, to Australia (Sydney), in October 1956, and to New York in 1960. Today, the country's flag carrier operates a large network of international scheduled passenger and cargo services from Bombay, Delhi, Calcutta, Trivandrum, Hyderabad, Goa and Madras to points in the Middle and Far East, Europe, Africa, Australia, the USA, and Canada. Services to Baghdad recommenced on August 14 1989. Wholly-owned subsidiaries are Air India Charters and the Hotel Corporation of India. The carrier also has holdings in the Indian regional airline, Vayudoot. A fleet of Airbus A300, A310 and Boeing 747 types are operated. In addition, one Ilyushin IL-62, one IL-76, and one Boeing 747-200F are leased-in. Currently on order are two Airbus A310-300s and four Boeing 747-400s. Depicted here on August 28 1975 is Boeing 707-337B, VT-DVA, 'Annapoorna'. The aircraft is seen on finals to London's Heathrow Airport. The airline's ICAO call sign is 'AIR INDIA'.

(B. J. Eagles)

AIR LANKA (UL/ALK)

Sri Lanka

Air Lanka was formed on January 30 1979, by the Sri Lankan Government, two national banks and the Ceylon Shipping Corporation, and began flight activities on September 1 of that year, with a leased Boeing 707 from Singapore Airlines. It was created to replace Air Ceylon, which terminated most international services in April 1978 on orders of the Sri Lankan Government (Air Ceylon has operated since 1949). Today the airline flies the flag of Sri Lanka on scheduled passenger services to points in Asia, as well as to Europe, from its base at Colombo. The current fleet consists of L-1011 TriStar's of various series, together with a sole Boeing 737 for domestic operations. An Airbus A320 will, however, replace this latter type, in the next year. Two Boeing 747s were purchased during the eighties, from Qantas, for use on services to Australia, but they proved to have an over capacity, so they were sold back to the Australian carrier. A bright red windowline runs from the nose and eventually encompasses the entire tail, forming the backdrop for the company's large white Peacock motif. The whole fuselage is finished in a fresh white with black 'Air Lanka' titles, alongside a representation of the Sri Lankan flag. Air Lanka is one of the few national carriers not to base its colour scheme on that of the country's flag, although the brown, red, green and yellow would probably not lend itself to a modern airliner.

AIR MAURITIUS (MK/MAU)   Mauritius

Air Mauritius was formed on June 14 1967, as a multi-national venture between the Mauritian Government, Rogers & Co, Air France and BOAC, later joined by Air India. It initially performed ground handling activities at Plaisance Airport, in Mauritius, and flew joint services with Air France, to Reunion Island (using Air France equipment). The airline commenced its own flights in August 1972 with a single leased Piper Navajo, flying to Rodrigues, but have since increased dramatically. As well as commuter flights linking the capital, Port Louis, with neighbouring islands, scheduled international services are operated to the Comoro Islands, Madagascar, Kenya and South Africa, and as far afield as Europe, flying to London (LHR), Rome, Frankfurt and Zurich, as well as to Bombay in India. For quite some years the airline made use of Twin Otters for local services and a Boeing 707, leased from British Airways, for international operations. However in 1983, two Boeing 707s were purchased from the Luxembourg airline, Luxair, and these were operated for sometime, until the introduction of the Boeing 767-200ERs which replaced them. Air Mauritius currently leases-in Boeing 747SP types from South African Airlines, and operates another, purchased from Aerolineas Argentinas. The first of these entered service in 1984, which took the airline into the wide-bodied era. The Mauritian flag carrier's livery is bright and cheerful. The fuselage of its aircraft, all white down to wing level, sports an attractive bright red windowline trimmed below with a similarly coloured pinstripe. Bold, upper case, red 'Air Mauritius' titles appear alongside the national flag. A bright red Falcon appears to 'hover' on the tail, within a white band across an otherwise predominantly red fin. the DHC-6 Twin Otters no longer appear in the fleet for domestic operations, having been replaced by the ATR 42, series 300.

AIR PORTUGAL — TAP (TP/TAP)

Portugal

Air Portugal was originally founded as Transportes Aereos Portugueses on March 14 1945, as a Special Department of the Secretariat for Civil Aviation; to carry out exploratory flights over potentially commercial routes such as Lisbon-Oporto, and to Portugal's African colonies. The airline commenced operations in September 1946 to Madrid, extended shortly afterwards to Angola and Mozambique, using Douglas DC-3s. It was nationalised in 1975. On May 3 1976, TAP began experimental third-level services within the Portuguese mainland, using Britten Norman Islander and Beech King Air types. Today, the Portuguese national carrier operates an extensive network of scheduled passenger and cargo services to Montreal, Toronto, Boston, New York (JFK), Los Angeles, Caracas, Recife, Rio de Janeiro, Sao Paulo, Kinshasa, Brazzaville, Harare, Abidjan, Dakar, Johannesburg, Luanda, Sal, Bissau, Maputo and throughout Europe, including new routes to Basle and Toulouse. Domestic flights serve Madeira, the Azores and, since 1989, Faro and Oporto. Other new destinations comprise Casablanca and Sao Tome, New York (EWR) and Curaçao. Air Portugal's aviation-related activities include Air Atlantis (charter services), LAR (dometic services), ESTA-Hotel Management, RN Tours and Air Portugal Tours. A fleet of Airbus Industrie A310, Boeing 727, 737, and Lockheed L-1011 Tristar 500 aircraft is maintained. Orders are outstanding for examples of the Boeing 737-500 and Airbus A340; deliveries of the latter will commence in 1993. The livery chosen to take the company into the eighties is based on a new style 'TAP' tail logo in red and white, whose red 'contrail' trimmed above in green extends along the fuselage from the cockpit windows to form the cheatline (at window level on the L-1011 Tristar, but lower on other types). Simple black 'Air Portugal' titling is displayed on the upper fuselage, which is white down to the wing level, where it becomes polished metal, or grey on the Airbus A310s. Seen here at Frankfurt Airport on August 6 1988 is CS-TBG, Boeing 707-382B. The carrier's ICAO call sign is 'TAP'. *(B. J. Eagles)*

AIR SEYCHELLES (HM/SEY)   Seychelles

Air Seychelles was originally founded as Seychelles Airlines on September 15 1977. However, the Seychellian Government formed the company in July 1979, when it acquired, and combined, Air Mahe (formed in early 1972 by John Falconer-Taylor, and started services with a Seneca in June of that year, between Mahe and Praslin), and Inter Island Airways (formed on August 12 1976, with a Britten-Norman fleet of one Islander and one Trislander). Today, the Government-owned national airline provides scheduled inter-island services between Mahe and the islands of Praslin, Fregate, Deroches, Bird and Denis. Photographic and sight-seeing tours are also operated. International scheduled services link Mahe with Paris (ORY), London (LGW), Frankfurt, Rome, Mauritius and Singapore. A fleet of Boeing 767, Boeing/De Havilland Canada DHC-6 Twin Otter, Britten-Norman Islander, and Dorner 228 aircraft is operated. The

Air Seychelles livery was introduced on November 1 1985, when the company leased-in an Airbus A300 from Air France for a short period. The specially-designed scheme consists of green stripes at the rear of an otherwise pure white fuselage. The red and green fin promotes silhouettes of two airborne gulls which are repeated on the engine cowlings. Blue 'Air Seychelles' titles are displayed on the upper fuselage, as is the national flag. Following the return of the A300, two hushkitted Boeing 707-300s (renamed 'Super Q's') were leased-in, but they too have left the fleet, to be replaced by a modern, wide-bodied jet in the shape of a Boeing 767-2Q8ER, which is being leased from the International Lease Finance Company, ILFC. The carrier's ICAO call sign is 'SEYCHELLES'.

(Author's Collection)

AIR ZIMBABWE (UM/AZW)   Zimbabwe

Air Zimbabwe was formed in September 1967 as Air Rhodesia, following the dissolution of Central African Airways Corporation (CAA), which had served the three territories of Southern Rhodesia, Nyasaland and Northern Rhodesia for a period of 21 years. During the 1970s, Rhodesia's racially-sparked political isolation compelled Air Rhodesia to gradually constrict its international system to a point where only South Africa was served. As Rhodesia headed towards black majority rule in 1979, the carrier's title became Air Zimbabwe-Rhodesia. Following Zimbabwean independence in 1980, the airline became Air Zimbabwe, and quickly re-established its links with states in southern Africa and Europe. Scheduled passenger and freight services link the capital, Harare, with neighbouring countries, as well as to Frankfurt, Athens and London (LGW) in Europe, to

Perth and Sydney in Australia. Domestic services connect all major cities and several important tourist attractions. A fleet of Boeing 707, 767, 737, Vickers Viscount and BAe 146 aircraft is operated. The latter is utilised on a share agreement with the Government of Zimbabwe. In early 1984, the somewhat sombre blue and white livery was exchanged for something totally different, and is exciting and dynamic as Africa itself. A quadruple cheatline in green, yellow, red and black flag colours commences at the nose and 'steps' up to the windowline ultimately embracing the tail fin, below a new star motif in yellow and red. Simple lower case 'Air Zimbabwe' lettering is displayed alongside a wavering portrayal of the national flag, near the forward passenger door.

ALYEMDA (DY/ALY)

South Yemen

Alyemda, the national airline of the People's Democratic Republic of Yemen (South Yemen), maintains regular scheduled passenger flights within the country, together with foreign points in the Middle East, East Africa, India and Europe. The carrier has been operating since March 11 1971, when it was established by Presidential decree. The new airline acquired a fleet of Douglas DC-3 and DC-6 types, and began scheduled operations from its base at Aden to points throughout the Middle East. Today scheduled Alyemda international services are operated from a main flight centre at Khormakear (the capital city's airport), with a secondary centre at Riyan. A mixed fleet of Western-built and Soviet aircraft is operated, this being made up of Antonov 12, Dash 7, Tupolev 154, Boeing 707 and 737 types.

AVIANCA COLOMBIA (AV/AVA)   Colombia

Avianca, Colombia's national carrier, has the distinction of being the oldest airline in the Americas. The company can trace its history back to 1919 when its predecessor, SCADTA, was formed by five Colombian and three German businessmen. Scheduled operations began in 1921 between Giradot (serving as the terminus for Bogota) and the Caribbean port of Barranquilla, with a fleet of German Junkers F13 float planes. In 1931 Pan American acquired an eighty per cent shareholding. Nine years passed and the present title was adopted when SCADTA merged with Servicio Aero Colombiano. 1954 saw Avianca take over the domestic carrier, SAETA, and by 1978 the company had bought outright Pan Am's original share-holding. Wholly-owned subsidiaries are Sociedade Aeronautica de Medellin (SAM) and Helicol. Today Avianca, based at Bogota's Eldorado Airport, operates an extensive domestic network, together with routes to Madrid, Paris (CDG), London (LGW) and Frankfurt in Europe; to Miami, New York (JFK), Los Angeles, Panama City, Mexico City and San Juan, Curaçao, Aruba, Port-au-Prince, and Santa Domingo in North and Central America; as well as to Quito, Lima, Santiago, Buenos Aires, Rio de Janeiro, Caracas and Montevideo in South America. The company maintains an all-Boeing fleet of 707, 727, 747 and 767 aircraft types. The company's livery is bright and somewhat distinctive, with the fuselage being painted in a warm red, in a 'dolphin' style unique to both Avianca and Iraqi Airways. This is designed to streamline the aircraft's overall appearance. 'Avianca Colombia' titles adorn the upper forward fuselage in white and black respectively, and the tail livery, redesigned in the early eighties, features red 'Avianca' lettering, which is underlined by a continuation of the fuselage cheatlines which colour the rear half of the fin. HK-1402, a Boeing 707-359B 'Sucre', is depicted here on arrival at Frankfurt Airport on October 26 1987. The airline's ICAO call sign is 'AVIANCA'. *(B. T. Richards)*

BIMAN BANGLADESH AIRLINES (BG/BBC)

Bangladesh

The national airline of Bangladesh was formed in January 1972, shortly after the country obtained its independence from Pakistan. Scheduled passenger services commenced in February of that year, with a DC-3 aircraft, and now connect the capital, Dhaka, with points in Europe, the Middle East and Asia, as well as linking several domestic cities. The first intercontinental flights linking the Bangladeshi capital with London (LHR), were initially operated with a Boeing 707-331, on wet lease from Tempair International Airlines. The modern western-built fleet employs four Douglas DC-10-30s on all long haul and high density routes, whilst Fokker F-28 and BAe ATPs fly on domestic and regional services. The introduction of Biman's first wide-bodied equipment in 1983 inspired Bangladesh

Airlines to update its livery to reflect that of a modern international flag carrier. Using the national colours of green and red, the company adopted a fashionable white overall finish which effectively modernised the appearance of the ageing Boeing 707s, in the fleet at that time, and provided a stylish new look to the DC-10s. The original design has since been slightly revised and now includes horizontal fin bands replacing the original vertical cheatline extension. Black titles are carried in English and Bengali on the port and starboard sides respectively, reading 'Bangladesh Airlines' on the forward upper cabin and 'Biman' on the raised engine. The motif, which represents a white stork flying across a setting sun, is displayed centrally on the motif.

BRITISH CALEDONIAN AIRWAYS (BR/BCA)

United Kingdom

British Caledonian Airways was formed on November 30 1970, when Caledonian Airways Limited, which had begun non-scheduled passenger and caro operations on November 30 1961 with one Douglas DC-7, took over British United Airways Ltd. The merger resulted from a recommendation by the Edwards Committee in 1969, that a 'second force' carrier should be established in order to provide competition for the then state-owned flag carrier, British Airways. It should be noted that the new airline was known as Caledonian/BUA until September 1 1972. Due to the report, a number of former BOAC international routes, mainly to Africa and South America, were transferred to BCAL operation. A further redistribution of routes was recommended by the Civil Aviation Authority in 1983 but, following the UK Government White Paper on 'Airline Competition Policy' in October 1984, only a relatively small exchange took place. The concept of a second-force UK scheduled airline had, by now, effectively been abandoned. BCAL had experienced over the past three years financial difficulties, and it became increasingly clear that, ultimately, it would be unlikely to remain a separate entity. Therefore, when the decision by British Airways was announced in December 1987 that it was to take over British Caledonian, it did not come as a truly great surprise. Scandinavian Airlines was, at one time, in the running to try and take over a large slice of the carrier; however, this was never to see the light of day. By April 1988 the company's scheduled services were operated under the BA name. Certain aspects of British Caledonian have been maintained by the formation of Caledonian Airways, which operates charter services formerly undertaken by British Airtours. Prior to the demise of BCAL, the airline maintained scheduled services to North America, North Africa, Europe, the Middle and Far East. A fleet of Douglas DC-10, Boeing 747, and BAe 1-11 aircraft was operated. Orders for the Airbus Industrie A320 were subsequently transferred to British Airways, however, delivery positions for an outstanding order for the McDonnell Douglas MD-11 were sold by BA to American Airlines. Two Airbus Industrie A310-203s were at one time operated by BCAL, but were sold, unknown to the company, to Libyan Arab Airlines. The highlight of the British Caledonian livery was the rampant heraldic lion which dominated the entire tail fin in gold, on a deep blue background. A dark blue windowline above a similar band in gold, separated the white upper and grey lower fuselage. Black 'British Caledonian' lettering is followed by the Union Flag on both sides of the fuselage, with the colloquial 'BCAL' logo and shield appearing on the engines of the A310s and DC-10s only. A Scottish flavour was maintained through the use of tartan uniforms and aircraft names, alongside small Scottish flags. Depicted here, on October 15, 1972, at London (LGW), is Boeing 707-365C, G-ATZC. The aircraft, 'County of Stirling', later renamed 'Loch Katrine', first flew on February 19 1967, and saw service with numerous carriers worldwide before being sold to Caledonian Airways in 1970. The aircraft is currently with Transbrasil, as PT-TCP. British Caledonian's ICAO call sign was 'CALEDONIAN'. (B. J. Eagles)

BRITISH MIDLAND (BD/BMA)　　United Kingdom

British Midland can trace its origins back to 1938, when Derby Aviation was formed. Scheduled services were introduced in 1953 and the name, British Midland Airways, was adopted in 1964. Minster Assets, an investment and banking group, acquired the airline in 1969, but in 1978 directors of the first carrier, headed by Michael Bishop, affected one of the first management buy-outs when they purchased the company. In 1982 British Midland and Air UK formed Manx Airlines to operate scheduled services from the Isle of Man. In 1983 Loganair was acquired from the Royal Bank of Scotland. Eurocity Express, since renamed London City Airways, was established in 1987 to operate from London's Dockland Airport. However, due to increasing financial debts and low passenger factors, the company ceased operations in 1990 and was merged into British Midland. Airlines of Britain Holding Plc was formed in March 1987 to act as a holding company for British Midland and its subsidiaries. The eighties also heralded a name change, to the present one. This was to underline the fact that the airline wanted to grow, but to offer an outstanding service and value for money. Today, British Midland operates a large network of scheduled services and is Heathrow's second-largest scheduled operator. In December 1988 SAS acquired a 24.9 per cent shareholding in the airline. British Midland's route network from Heathrow includes Amsterdam, Paris (CDG), Belfast, Dublin, East Midlands, Edinburgh, Glasgow, Liverpool, Leeds/Bradford, Nice, Palma and Teesside. The company plans to expand its Heathrow operations considerably and has received approvals for a substantial number of routes. British Midland's other main routes include East Midlands to Amsterdam, Belfast, Glasgow and Paris (CDG), as well as Birmingham to Brussels and Berlin. The airline has also been for many years a major operator to the Channel Islands. On many of its routes high quality 'Diamond Service' is offered, for which the company has received wide acclaim. Inclusive-tour charter flights are also operated. A fleet of Douglas DC-9, Boeing 737 and British Aerospace ATP types are operated. Seen here is one of the company's Boeing 707s that it used to operate on services that included East Midlands to New York (JFK). Nowadays, the aircraft have gone and the route has been dropped. The carrier's ICAO call sign is 'MIDLAND'. *(K. G. Wright)*

BURLINGTON AIR EXPRESS (FR)

United States of America

Burlington Northern Air Freight, formed at the end of 1985, is an airfreight forwarder with its own aircraft. All of which are contracted out and are operated on behalf of Burlington Air Express. It is one of the latest airlines to enter into the US small parcels market. Scheduled freight services are offered throughout the United States of America, with main hubs in Michigan, Florida and Texas. World-wide charters are also undertaken, with the aircraft being frequently seen in the United Kingdon. The entire fleet, which comprises of Douglas DC-8, Boeing 757 and Boeing 707 types, sport the carrier's full colours and titles. This comprises of bright yellow and dark green, which colour the triple cheatlines. These extend along the entire length of the pure-white fuselage, interrupted by bold green 'Burlington Air Express' titling. The all-white tail fin displays the simple 'BN' motif of the company's parent, Burlington Northern. It should be noted that the aircraft registration is carried in green at the base of the fin. The following companies maintain the aircraft: Amerijet, Buffalo Airways, Rosenbalm Aviation and Southern Air Transport. Depicted here is N864BX, a Boeing 707-321C, during March 1986. The aircraft, c/n 19375, made its maiden flight on December 24 1967, and was delivered to Pan American World Airways in January of the following year as N473PA, 'Clipper Pride of America'. Following a period of over twenty years uninterrupted service, the 707 left the US carrier's fleet, and was sold to Ronair Inc. The same day that the aircraft was sold, it was leased to Iran Air; and in December 1978 was reregistered N473RN. 'Romeo November' was returned to Ronair in 1979 and was leased to Trans Cargo in February of the following year. Following its return, the 707 was purchased by a company called ATASCO Leasing, and leased to Avianca as HK-2473, with whom it stayed for two years. Faucett of Peru then operated the aircraft as OB-R-1243. Following a further series of leases, the aircraft ended up with Burlington Air Express as N864BX. *(Author's Collection)*

CYPRUS AIRWAYS (CY/CYP)

Cyprus

The tiny Mediterranean island of Cyprus employs a modern international flag carrier to connect with the rest of the world. Scheduled passenger and freight services link Larnaca with major cities throughout Europe and the Middle East. Cyprus Airways' fleet is now one of the most modern in the world, comprising of the Airbus A310 and A320 types. The former having replaced the older, and noisier, Boeing 720s, whilst the latter has replaced the Boeing 707s and BAe 1-11s operated by the airline. Although at the time of writing a new livery was due to be implemented, the current colour scheme chosen for the airline of a sunshine island deserved to be a little brighter, but the overall livery is stylish and 'up to the minute'. Twin royal blue cheatlines originate at the nose and widen as they proceed along the fuselage length, separated by an autumn gold line. The tail is finished in royal blue, a continuation of the upper cheatline, promoting the company motif in the form of a white winged mountain goat caricature. Royal blue 'Cyprus Airways' lettering in the traditional style appears behind the forward passenger door. The airline was formed in September 1947, with the initial shareholders being British European Airways, the Cypriot Government, and local interests. In April of the following year, the carrier acquired three Douglas DC-3 Dakotas, and opened routes between Nicosia and Beirut, Cairo, Haifa, Istanbul, Rome and Athens. During the 1950s and 60s, the airline greatly expanded its operations, and added turboprop, and laterm jet equipment, to its fleet. In July 1974, a Cypriot war was sparked by a coup and Turkish military invasion. The airline had one Trident jetliner destroyed and its four other aircraft trapped at Nicosia International Airport. Operations were fully suspended for seven months. On February 8 1975, the carrier resumed activities from a new base at Larnaca, on the southern coast of Cyprus. Tremendous growth has taken place since the war, and the airline is today totally revitalised.

DAIRO AIR SERVICES (SE/DSR)　　　Uganda

Dairo Air Services, or DAS Air Cargo, the Ugandan all-cargo carrier, was formed in 1983 as a subsidiary of GAS Air Cargo of Nigeria, and provides scheduled and charter cargo services between Europe and East and West Africa from its base at Entebbe. The company maintains its sales and operations office in the UK. Boeing 707-300C aircraft are leased-in from the parent company as needs require. The DAS Air Cargo livery is closely based on that of GAS Air Cargo, although there are one or two minor adjustments. The red 'Air Cargo' element of the roof-titling arrangement has been retained, but with the original word 'GAS', which appeared in red, white and blue horizontal stripes, simply replaced by 'DAS' in red matching letters. Triple cheatlines in red, yellow and brown are unchanged, but the all-white fin now sports a rather dormant-looking antelope motif in place of the parent company's impressive 'leaping-lion' design. Boeing 707-321C, 5X-DAR, can be seen here

whilst taxiing at Geneva's Cointrin Airport. The aircraft was transporting cargo from its Entebbe base. 'Alpha Romeo" c/n 18825, made its inaugural flight on August 14 1964, and should have been delivered to Pam American World Airways as N798PA. This order was never taken up, and instead the aircraft was delivered to Continental Air Lines as N17321 on August 21 that year. The American carrier made good use of the 707 until May 1973, when it was sold it to China Airlines as B-1832. From there the aircraft spent the next twelve years in the Far East, before being sold to Allen Aircraft Corporation as N987AA. GAS Air Nigeria then purchased the aircraft as 5X-DAR in February 1986, before leasing it to Dairo Air Services the same day. In January 1988, Equator Leasing purchased the 707, and leased the aircraft back to the Ugandan airline. The carrier's ICAO call sign is 'DAIRAIR'. *(R. Von Arx)*

DAN AIR SERVICES (DA/DAN) United Kingdom

Dan Air is the airline and engineering subsidiary of Davies and Newman Holdings Plc, London shipping brokers and travel group (established in 1922), from which its name is derived. The carrier was founded on May 21 1953. Although scheduled services were started in 1959, the company specialised mainly in general charter work and during the sixties and seventies developed extensive inclusive-tour operations using a fleet of Comet aircraft. One-elevens and Boeing 727s were later added. Transatlantic charter flights to the United States were introduced on April 1 1971, although these were stopped when Dan Air sold its Boeing 707s. Following the acquisition of Skyways International, all scheduled activities were operated under the title of Dan Air Skyways, but this was subsequently dropped late in 1973. The company is a major operator of scheduled passenger services and is the UK's second-largest scheduled carrier to international destinations. The airline is also a major operator of inclusive-tour flights to resorts throughout Europe, the Mediterranean, the Canary Islands, and the Middle East, from more than a dozen airports in the UK, under contract to most British tour operators. Similar services are provided for German tour operators from West Berlin. Dan Air also maintains contract services for oil companies, together with ad hoc passenger and cargo charters and night mail contracts. The scheduled network includes services from London (Heathrow) to Inverness, London (Gatwick) to Aberdeen, Berne, Brussels, Gibraltar, Ibiza, Innsbruck, Inverness, Jersey, Lisbon, Lourdes, Madrid, Mahon, Manchester, Montpellier, Newcastle, Nice, Paris (CDG), Perpignan, Toulouse, West Berlin and Zurich; Manchester and Newcastle to Amsterdam, Bergen, Oslo and Stavanger; Manchester to Montpellier; Leeds/Bradford, and Newcastle to Jersey; Teesside to Amsterdam; Berlin to Amsterdam and Saarbrucken; Aberdeen to Inverness, Manchester and Newcastle; Manchester to Berne and Inverness, and Jersey to Cork. Future route developments for which Dan Air is already licensed include Gatwick to Alicante, Santiago de Compostela and Seville, and Manchester to Goteborg. Dan Air's engineering division maintains the carrier's own fleet of aircraft and undertakes third-party contract maintenance and overhaul for other airlines at its three bases: Lasham, Manchester and Gatwick. Subsidiary companies include Gatwick Handling, Manchester Handling. Other subsidiaries of Davies and Newman Holdings Plc include shipbrokers and ships' agents and travel. The carrier operates a fleet of BAe 146, 748, 1-11, Boeing 727 and 737 types. When the old red and black livery was finally dropped with the Comets, Dan Air chose a totally fresh image to take it into the eighties. Blue and red from the national flag colour the dual dart cheatlines which originate at the nose and fan out along the fuselage length, ultimately encompassing most of the tail where they form the traditional compass and penant motif. Black 'Dan Air London' lettering is preceded by the Union Flag on the upper forward fuselage on the port side, and follows the lettering on the starboard. Depicted here at Gatwick, on October 15 1972, is Boeing 707-321, G-AYSL. The aircraft is seen sporting a previous livery. The carrier's ICAO call sign is 'DAN AIR'.
(B. J. Eagles)

DOMINICANA (DO/DOA)   Dominican Republic

Dominicana was founded in 1944 by a group of businessmen, headed by Guillermo Santoni Calero (with 60% share ownership) and Pan American (with 40%). The first service was opened on July 5 of that year from the capital, Ciudad Trujilo (now Santo Domingo), to La Tomana and Santiago de Los Caballeros, using two Ford Tri-motors leased from Cubana de Aviacion. Today the company is wholly owned by the state financial institution, Corporacion Dominicana de Empresas Estatalas. Scheduled operations link Santo Domingo with Curaçao, Caracas (in association with Viasa), Aruba, Port-au-Prince, Miami, San Juan and New York (JFK). In addition to these, a network of domestic destinations is also maintained. Charter flights are also flown throughout the Caribbean area. A fleet of Boeing 707, 727 and C-118A (Douglas DC-6) aircraft are operated. Until fairly recently, the flagship of the airline was a Boeing 747, which it leased from Citicorp. The aircraft was used on high-density routes, including long haul charters to Europe. Dominicana's Boeing 707 and 727s fly most of the regional services, whilst the

company's ageing C-118A is kept solely for the movement of freight. The airline's livery is bright and distinctive as well as being rather ingenious. Twin cheatlines in red and blue, separated by a narrow white line, extend along the fuselage and up onto the tail, where they form the national flag of red and blue quarters, divided by a white cross. Bold 'Dominicana' roof titling in black is worn above the wing on the DC-6, so as to avoid obliteration by the open cargo door whilst loading, but appears further forward, near the main passenger door, on the other types. It should be noted that although both the DC-6 and Boeing 707 feature a white cabin roof, the 727s are in the same livery but with a natural-metal fuselage finish. The leased Boeing 747 wore a hybrid livery with a dark blue cheatline over a natural metal. Seen here at the Miami International Airport, Florida, is the company's sole Boeing 707-399C, HI-442. It should be noted that during Feburary 1989 the aircraft was re-registered as HI-442CT. The carrier's ICAO call sign is 'DOMINICANA'.

(Author's Collection)

DONALDSON INTERNATIONAL AIRWAYS

United Kingdom

Donaldson International Airways was formed in the 1960s as a charter and inclusive-tour passenger carrier. The company also offered worldwide freight charter services. Utilising a fleet of Boeing 707 and Bristol Britannia aircraft, the carrier maintained a route network of transatlantic services throughout Canada and the USA from its base at London Gatwick. However, Glasgow and other regional airports were often used, as demand dictated. Points within Europe and the Far East were also operated to, as and when operations required. Unfortunately, due to a slump in demand for package holidays and the increase in the price of fuel, Donaldson was forced to close in the early seventies, thus becoming a victim of the 'holiday war', which is still going on. The aircraft depicted here, G-AYXR, Boeing 707-321, is seen at London's Gatwick on October 30 1971. As construction number 17608, it had made its maiden flight on

April 15 1960, before being delivered shortly after to Pan American World Airways as N730PA, 'Clipper Bald Eagle'. Donaldson International Airways purchased the 707 in December 1970 and converted it to a Series 321F the same month. Following this it was re-registered G-AYXR and plyed the airline's routes worldwide. The aircraft was named 'Mikado II' in May of the following year, just prior to Donaldson ceasing all operations. 'X-Ray Romeo' was subsequently repossessed by Pan Am in August 1974 before it was sold to the Continental Illinois Bank in February of the following year. The aircraft then saw service with various airlines throughout the world, including such companies as British Midland, Syrian Arab, Tunis Air and Pakistan International. It was stored at Lasham for a period of two years, before being leased in 1983 to General Electric, who then purchased the 707 in 1986. *(B. J. Eagles)*

ECUATORIANA (EU/EEA)   Ecuador

Ecuatoriana was formed in July 1974 as the national airline of Ecuador, and took over the operating rights, debts and assets of the private airline, Compania Ecuatoriana de Aviacion (CEA). CEA had been formed in February 1957 by a group of local businessmen, who subscribed 81% of the capital, and an American citizen, Elly Hecksher. Operations began in the latter part of the year, from Quito and Guayaquil to Miami, with Curtiss C-46s. The Government of Ecuador gained limited control of the carrier in 1972, and full control in 1974. Today the airline operates scheduled passenger services from Quito and Guayaquil to New York (JFK), Los Angeles, Chicago, Caracas, Santiago, Panama City, Cali, Lima, Mexico City, Bogota, Rio de Janeiro, San Jose and Bueno Aires; and an all-cargo service to Miami, Panama City and New York (JFK). Engineering and technical support is provided under contract by Israel Aircraft Industries. A fleet of Boeing 707 and Douglas DC-10 aircraft is maintained. The last three Boeing 720s were withdrawn from use during December 1985, and were stored at the Marana Air Park, pending sale. Although something of a departure from the flamboyant Indian style schemes of the seventies, the current Ecuatoriana livery is widely regarded as one of the world's most flamboyant, and dare it be said, attractive, promoting a stylish and distinctive company image. An all-cream fuselage forms the backdrop for six bands of bright colour, yellow, green and blue sweeping down from the cabin roof, and magenta, orange and red rising from the fuselage undersides; the resulting six-part cheatline continues along the rear of the fuselage and flows up onto the tail, where it is surmounted by the company's traditional 'E' motif in black and white. All of the passenger Boeing 707 aircraft in the fleet, including the Douglas DC-10, now wear this standard livery. However, the 707 freighter, HC-BGP, 'Manabi', as depicted here, sports a unique gold fuselage finish, standard six-part cheatlines and additional 'Ecuatoriana Jet Cargo' titling and freight motif in black. The carrier's ICAO call sign is 'ECUATORIANA'. *(Author's Collection)*

EGYPTAIR (MS/MSR)

Egypt

Egyptair was originally founded in June 1932 as Misr Airwork. With technical and operational assistance from Airwork, services commenced in July 1933, between Cairo and Mersa Matruh, via Alexandria, using a fleet of de Havilland DH 84 Dragon Rapides. This was followed the year after by an international route to Lydda and Haifa. The name Misrair was adopted in 1949, and it was not until many years of operation under the name of United Arab Airlines, that the company adopted the present title on October 10 1971. Under both titles, the livery used consisted basically of a green cheatline with slight variations over the years. the Antonov An-24 aircraft introduced in the mid-sixties, carried a red, white, black livery of the national colours. The current international scheduled passenger network includes major cities in Europe, the Middle East, Far East and Africa, as well as domestic services, operated under the name of Air Sinai. Long-haul routes are served by wide-bodied Boeing 747s, 767s and Airbus A300s, supported by Boeing 707s, with Boeing 737s and Airbus A320s, being used on domestic and regional flights. The hawk head of Horus, the omnipotent Falcon-headed god of ancient Egypt, is displayed in red and black within a gold disk on the tail fin, and repeated on the engines. A broad windowline takes its colour from the Egyptian flag and runs from the nose and all the way up the tail, above a narrower line in gold. Black 'Egyptair' titles in English and Arabic, separated by the Egyptian flag, decorate the forward upper fuselage. Boeing 767s display an attractive highly-polished lower body, but this is left natural metal or grey, on other types.

FAST AIR CARRIER (UD/FST)

Chile

Fast Air was formed on August 14 1978 by a group of Chilean businessmen in limited partnership, and began operations on November 27 of that year. Today the Chilean operator provides cargo charters throughout the world from its Santiago base, but principally throughout North and South America. In addition scheduled services link the nation's capital with Bogota (Colombia), Frankfurt (West Germany), Miami and New York (JFK) (USA), Panama City (Panama), and Sao Paulo (Brazil). The airline maintains two Boeing 707-331C Freighters. The first, CC-CAF, c/n 19435, depicted here, was the original aircraft to join the fleet and was, until recently, the sole plane to be operated by Fast Air. It had been supplied by Trans World Airlines, just prior to the Chilean company's launch. The plane was originally registered N5774T. CC-CUE

on the other hand, is currently being leased from RACE Inc (see separate entry). It was originally registered N345FA, and has construction number 20069. A new corporate image was adopted in the mid-eighties, when the 707 received a new paint scheme, replacing the original two-tone blue cheatlines. The pure-white fuselage now sports triple 'chin' bands in dark blue, green and pale blue, repeated under the tail section, and simple 'Fast Air' roof titling preceded by a company motif, representing the letter 'F'. This was the previous scheme's centrepiece, where it dominated the tail. Under the new design, the fin is painted deep blue, promoting white 'Fast Air' titles in a style which matches those of the fuselage. The carrier's ICAO call sign is 'FASTER'. *(Author's Collection)*

FLORIDA WEST AIRLINES (HG/FWL)

United States of America

Florida West Airlines, based at Miami, Florida, was formed in April 1983 and now offers freight services on both a scheduled and charter basis, weekly to Colombia and twice weekly to Guatemala, Costa Rica, Panama and the Lesser Antilles. In addition, it runs a 707/720 repair station at Miami. The airline, formerly known as Pan Aero International, and as Aero Exchange, gained charter authority from the Civil Aeronautics Board in 1981 and received domestic scheduled rights in 1984. Florida West's fleet consists entirely of second-hand Boeing 707-300Cs. At one stage it was hoped that the carrier would commence domestic military contract charters, as well as services to Europe, but these never materalised. There was also a possibility that a Boeing 747 might join the fleet, but again this never happened. During the early years of the carrier's existence, Florida West had proposed scheduled low-fare passenger jet services between such cities as Baltimore, Charleston (South Carolina), Hartford, Houston, Miami, Orlando and Tampa. Equipment that was to be used was the twin engined Boeing 737. International services were also proposed to the Bahamas, Mexico, and various Caribbean islands. Unfortunately, however, permission was not granted and th airline has maintained its position of being a cargo airline. Florida West's livery is worn by the entire fleet. This features triple cheatlines in bright 'sunshine state' colours of yellow, orange and red, commencing below the cockpit windows, rising at an angle in line with the wing and ultimately connecting with the horizontal stabilisers at the rear. Bold 'Florida West' titling is displayed on the bare metal cabin roof, mostly in red script but with the letter 'F' in yellow and orange. The fin sports a repeat of the company's 'FW' initials in a similar style to those on the fuselage. The carrier's ICAO call sign is 'FLO WEST'. *(Author's Collection)*

GAS AIR CARGO (GS/NGS)   Nigeria

GAS Air Cargo, or to give the airline its full title, General And Aviation Services Limited, is a Nigerian freight operator which offers local cargo charters in addition to a regular service from the capital, Lagos, to Entebbe (Uganda), Dar-es-Salaam (Tanzania), and Amsterdam (Netherlands). The carrier commenced operations in October 1983 following the purchase of its first aircraft, 5N-ARQ, a Boeing 707-338C freighter; the plane having been obtained from International Air Leases. Although no longer the present livery, the GAS Air colour scheme consisted of 'straight through', below window cheatlines coloured in red, yellow and brown, to match the tail motif of a leaping lion and a winged globe, which looked very much like a tennis ball. 'Gas Air Cargo' roof titles featured the first word in red, white and blue stripes, though 'Air' and 'Cargo' were in bigger, solid red letters. Today the livery has changed greatly. Windowlevel 'straight through' cheatlines in red and black taper at the front, behind a black nose cone. Red 'Gas Air Cargo' roof titles

are situated towards the front of the aircraft. A continuation of the cheatlines is situated at the bottom of the tail, whilst a new tail logo has been adopted. A large 'G' encompasses the letters 'A' and 'S' to form a more modern image. 5N-AYJ, a Boeing 707-351C, is seen here sporting the current livery. The aircraft, c/n 19168, made its maiden flight on July 1 1966, and was delivered later that month to Northwest Orient as N367US. It remained with the company for seven years, before being sold to Bangladesh Biman as S2-ABN, who named the aircraft 'Land of Shah Jalal'. In 1976 it was renamed 'City of Shah Jalal'. Tempair International purchased the plane in April 1988, followed by its sale to Fast Cargo Airways in June of that year. 5N-AYJ was leased to GAS Air Cargo on the same day. However, six months later, the 707 was on a regular flight when it crashed at Kom-Omran, some 65 kilometres south of Luxor, Egypt.

(Author's Collection)

HANG KHONG VIETNAM (VN/HVN)   Vietnam

Domestic air services within the Southeast Asian Socialist Republic of Vietnam are performed by the state-owned national carrier, Hang Khong Vietnam, and link Hanoi with Ho Chi Minh City, Dien Bien, Na San, Yen Bai, Lao Cai, Cao Bang, Vinh, Hue, Da Nong, Play Ku, Da Lat, Buon Me Thuot, Nha Trang, Qui Nhon, Phu Quoc, Rach Gia, Hau Giang, Ca Mau and Con Son. International sectors connect Vietnam's capital with several important regional cities, including Vientiane (Laos), Bangkok (Thailand) and Phnomh Penh (Kampuchea). The airline was established in 1976, subsequent to the unification of Vietnam, to succeed Hanoi-based CAAV, the Civil Aviation Administration of Vietnam. The new carrier also took over remaining facilities and abandoned aircraft of Air Vietnam, the former South Vietnamese carrier. Flights to the Thai capital commenced on May 22 1978, when a 50-seat Antonov An-24V was used. The airline took

over Aeroflot's rights on the Hanoi–Vientiane route on December 1 1976. A predominantly, Soviet-supplied fleet including Tupolev Tu-134s, Yakovlev Yak-40s, Ilyushin Il-18s, Antonov An-24s, An-26s, and Boeing 707s, make up the mainstay of the fleet. Modern western-built aircraft have been leased-in to 'upgrade' the 'Soviet'-style service, offered by the airline. Although a different livery has now been introduced, the one depicted here is almost indistinguishable from that of Aeroflot, with its double mid-blue cheatline and red tail flag, though the flag is that of Vietnam rather than Russia. However, the Vietnamese carrier's roof titles are considerably more impressive than the simple 'Aeroflot', stating 'Hang Khong Viet Nam', in bold blue titles complete with no less than three accents. A 'winged star' company motif, located for'ard of the titles, is based closely on the 'winged hammer and sickle' of the Russian airline.

IRAQI AIRWAYS (IA/IAW)   Iraq

Iraqi Airways was founded in December 1945 by the Iraqi State Railways. The company inaugurated its first service on January 29 1946, between Baghdad and the main port of Basra, using de Havilland Dragon Rapides; international flights began on June 14 of that year, between Baghdad and Damascus. Vickers Viscount turboprop aircraft were introduced in 1957, followed by Hawker Siddeley Trident jets in 1965, Boeing 707s and 737s in 1974, and Boeing 727s and 747s in 1976. Today, Iraqi Airways operates scheduled passenger and cargo services from its base at Baghdad to points in the Middle East, Europe, Asia and North Africa. A domestic network linking Baghdad, Mosul and Basra is also undertaken. The airline maintains a fleet of Boeing 707, 727, 737, 747, Ilyushin IL-76, Antonov An-12, AN-24, Jetstar II, Falcon 50, Piaggio P.166 and Tupolen TU-124 aircraft types. In July 1990 Iraq invaded Kuwait. Many of the aircraft were subsequently possessed on behalf of Iraqi Airways. The distinctive 'Dolphin style' two tone green livery, pioneered by Iraqi Airways, was introduced by the carrier in November 1974. A conventional bright green cheatline is worn at windowlevel, but above this the fuselage roof is coloured in dark green, tapering at the 'waist' and sweeping up to encompass the tail fin. White 'Iraqi Airways' fuselage titling is carried on the starboard side in English, and the port side in Koufai, with the lettering on the tail reading 'Iraqi' in the opposite language to that on the fuselage. Therefore, both languages are represented on each side. The dark green Iraqi Airways stylised bird motif, believed to be of ancient Mesopotamian origin, appears in a white disk on the fin. It should be noted that although the livery described here is worn by all the commercial aircraft, government and military transports usually sport varying hybrid finishes in white and grey, with green 'Iraqi Airways' titles and logo and a more prominent national flag. Depicted here is one of the company's Boeing 707s on approach to London's Heathrow Airport. The carrier's ICAO call sign is 'IRAQI'.
(K. G. Wright)

J.A.T. — YUGOSLAV AIRLINES (JU/JAT)

Yugoslavia

JAT was formed by the Yugoslavian Government on April 1 1947, to take-over from the Yugoslav Air Force, the operations of domestic and international passenger services using two Junkers Ju-52s and two Douglas DC-3s. Flights began the same day, over Belgrade–Zagreb–Ljubljana and Zagreb–Sarajevo routes, and the international Belgrade–Prague–Warsaw service. Its predecessor, known as Aeroput, was founded in 1927. In 1949, JAT took over the routes and some personnel from the joint Yugoslav-Soviet company JUSTA (established in 1946 with a fleet of Lisunov Li-2's). Today, the state-owned carrier flies scheduled services to all major European destinations, plus points in North America, the Middle East, Africa, the Far East and Australia. As well as these operations, JAT undertakes extensive charter services, through a subsidiary known as Air Yugoslavia. In addition, a comprehensive domestic network is maintained and two separate divisions provide air-taxi and agricultural services. A western-built fleet consists of Boeing 727, 737, Douglas DC-9, DC-10 and MD-11 types. As with many national airlines, the colours of the flag are widely employed providing the blue and red of the cheatlines. The starboard fuselage features English 'Yugoslav Airlines' titling with 'Jugoslavenski Aerotransport' appearing on the port. The traditional red and white "JAT" logo has remained unchanged and is displayed prominently on the mainly blue fin. A sparkling new livery was introduced during August 1985 to coincide with the delivery of the first Boeing 737-300, featuring a highly polished natural metal fuselage and a more modern, below window cheatline arrangement. It should be noted that this livery has not been placed on any other type in the fleet.

KENYA AIRWAYS (KQ/KQA)   Kenya

The collapse of the joint venture, East African Airways, in 1976, persuaded the Kenyan Government to form its own national flag carrier, to be responsible not only for providing an international air link, but also to connect several widespread domestic communities. International scheduled services commenced on January 22, 1977, under the name of Kenya Airways, using Boeing 707s leased from British Midland Airways. Subsequent to its scheduled jet flight inaugural between Nairobi and London (LHR) on February 4 of that year, Kenya Airways quickly developed a substantial intercontinental route system, to emerge as a prominent East African carrier. Today, it now connects Nairobi with major points in

Europe, the Middle East and Africa. A Kenya Airways subsidiary is Kenya Flamingo Airways, a charter division which has been inactive for several years. A fleet of Boeing 707, 720, 757, Airbus A310 and Fokker 50 aircraft is utilised. The triple cheatline, taking its colours from the black, red and green of the national flag, runs along the fuselage length, with the red central windowline extended at the front, to reach the cockpit windows. Simple black 'Kenya Airways' titling is worn on the cabin roof and the white tail displays a specially-designed 'KA' motif in red within a black outline disk.

KUWAIT AIRWAYS (KU/KAC)   Kuwait

Kuwait Airways, the country's national flag carrier, was formed in March 1954 by a group of local businessmen under the name Kuwait National Airways Company. Its aim was to operate a fleet of Douglas DC-3s between Kuwait and Basrah. By mid-1955 the Kuwaiti Government had gained a 50% holding in the carrier, and the airline was renamed the Kuwait Airways Company three years later. British Overseas Airways Corporation took over technical management under a five-year contract in May 1958, and British International Airlines was completely absorbed in April 1959. The carrier became wholly Government-owned in July 1962. In March 1964 the airline commenced Comet jet flights to Europe, and the following month absorbed Trans Arabian Airways. Today the carrier provides scheduled passenger and cargo services from Kuwait to forty-one cities in thirty-eight countries in the Middle and Far East, Europe, North Africa and North America. Subsidiaries include Kuwait Aviation Services Company — KASCO — a catering firm. A fleet of Boeing 727, 747, 767, Airbus A300 and A310 aircraft is maintained. BAe 125–700s and Gulfstream 3s are used on purely VIP and executive flights. The original livery utilised by Kuwait Airways when the airline was first formed in 1954 comprised a light blue cheatline with an all blue fin with two horizontal white bands. The airline logo appeared in English and Arabic in red. This livery was applied to the first jet airliners in the fleet, the de Havilland Tridents, but on delivery of the company's Boeing 707 fleet a new livery appeared. This comprised an attractive shade of ocean blue which was chosen as the colour to adorn the windowline and tail band, trimmed either side in black in both cases. The latter contains the company's stylised bird logo. English and Arabic titling reads 'Kuwait Airways' in blue, giving precedence to the latter language on the starboard side and the former on the port. Tail lettering in separate languages appears on either side. The national flag appears at the top of the tail. Depicted here whilst on approach to London's Heathrow Airport is one of Kuwait Airways' Boeing 707 aircraft, it having operated a service from Kuwait, via Geneva. Although no longer with the company, the type provided the airline with a strong workhorse to utilise. The carrier's ICAO call sign is 'KUWAITI'. During the invasion of Kuwait by Iraq, the latter country has ceased to recognise Kuwait Airways as an airline and merged the airline's entire fleet with its own. However, following the implementation of Allied troops, Iraq returned the airline and its aircraft to Kuwait, albeit minus a few 'written off' types. In 1991, KAC placed a large order with Airbus Industrie, for the purchase of over twenty various Airbus types, for delivery in the mid-nineties.

(Author's Collection)

LAN CHILE (LA/LAN)
Chile

LAN-Chile was founded by the Chilean Government on March 5 1929 under the command of the Chilean Air Force. Originally known as Linea Aeropostal Santiago-Africa, the airline took its present title in 1932, when it became an autonomous state entity. With a fleet of twelve de Havilland 'Gypsy Moth' bi-planes, the carrier opened a mail service from Santiago to Africa in the far north of the country, and this was followed by the first external flight across the Andes to Mendoza and San Juan in the Argentine. LAN-Chile was privatised in September 1989. It became the first ever airline to undertake a twinjet (Boeing 767) revenue service across the South Atlantic, from Rio de Janeiro to Madrid, in September 1986. In 1974 the carrier was the first to link South America with Australia via the South Pole, an 11 hour 16 minute experimental flight. LAN-Chile operates a large network of international passenger and cargo services from its Santiago base, to Buenos Aires, Montevideo, Sao Paulo, Caracas, Rio de Janeiro, Lima, La Paz, Miami, New York (JFK), Montreal, Los

Angeles, Panama, Madrid, Papeete and Santa Cruz. Domestic flights are also operated to Africa, Iquique, Calama, Antofagasta, El Salvador, Concepcion, Puerto Montt, Punta Arenas, Temuco, Copiapo, Easter Island (Rapa Nui), La Serena, Coyhaique, Osorno and Valdiva. A fleet of Boeing 707, 737, 767 and BAe 146 aircraft is operated. A Boeing 747-100 is leased-in for the summer season, and an order is currently outstanding for three examples of the Boeing 767-300ER. LAN-Chile's colour scheme is made up from patriotic shades of red, white and blue, which make up the triple cheatline that commences under the nose and continues along the fuselage, ultimately encompassing the entire fin. 'LAN-Chile' titling is displayed in white on the tail, reversed out of the blue, and in red on the forward cabin roof, alongside a white star in a red and blue disk. It should be noted that the Chilean flag appears under the cockpit windows. Depicted here is a 707-321B, CC-CEK at Miami on 10 April 1989. *(W. Kathe)*

LIBYAN ARAB AIRLINES (LN/LAA)   Libya

The national airline of the Socialist People's Libyan Arab Jamahiriya, was formed in 1964 as a Government Corporation under the Ministry of Communciations with the title Royal Libyan Airlines to succeed NAA Libiavia. Domestic passenger services were commenced in October of the following year, as Kingdom of Libya Airlines. The present title was adopted following Libya's revolution in September 1969, and today the company provides domestic scheduled services connecting Tripoli with nine other major towns. International routes link Tripoli, Benghazi and Sebha with Algiers, and to various points throughout Europe. Services to London (LHR) were suspended following the cessation of diplomatic relations, during the eighties. A mixture of Western and Soviet-built aircraft are operated by the airline. These include Boeing 707, 727, Fokker F-27, Twin Otter, Gulfstream 2, and Ilyushin Il-76 types. The Libyan Arab Airlines livery is a tasteful blend of gold (symbolising quality) and chocolate brown, with a simple gold windowline and tail fin. The strange tail motif, designed by a Libyan artist, appears to be three brown arrows, but actually they represent the Uaddan, a rare type of deer found in Libya, leaping an obstruction, the upper arrow. The lower arrow represents the horizon. The colour of the motif is burnt sienna — the exact colour of the fertile soil of Barce — the most fertile and productive in the country. The emblem as a whole is intriguing and induce one to read the name written on the aircraft's upper fuselage, which appears on the port side in Arabic script, and on the starboard in English. The logo is preceded by the Libyan national flag. It should be noted that the domestic Fokker F-27s wear brown fuselage titling in Arabic only.

LUFTHANSA (LH/DLH)   Germany

The national flag carrier of Germany operates a vast route network of scheduled passenger and freight services. Over 120 destinations are served within 71 countries on all five continents. The airline can trace its history back to January 6 1926, when Deutsch Luft Hansa was formed through a merger of Aero Lloyd and Junkers Luftverkehr (Aero Lloyd began operations as Deutsche Luftreederel in January 1919, from Hamburg to Amsterdam and Copenhagen). The new carrier began flights on April 6 1926, followed by night operations between Berlin and Konigsberg, on May 1. Following World War II, this original Luft Hansa was dissolved. In 1953 a new West German national airline was established, known as Luftag. The company was renamed Deutsche Lufthansa in August 1954. Domestic flights started on April 1 1955, with a fleet of Convair 340 twin-engined airlines. International services added a month later. Today, a fleet of Boeing 727, 737, 747, 757 (operated by the company's subsidiary, Condor), Airbus A300, A310, A320 and Douglas DC-10 is maintained.

Orders for the A321 and A340 remain outstanding, for delivery during the mid-1990s. During the eighties, a series of experimental liveries were tested out on various aircraft. However, the one that was finally chosen, was not a million miles away from that seen depicted here on this Boeing 707. The tail logo and colouring remain the same, whilst an all white fuselage is now the order of the day, with large blue 'Lufthansa' titling on the forward fuselage.

MALAYSIA-SINGAPORE AIRLINES (ML)

Malaysia/Singapore

During the first half of 1966 the management of Malaysian Airways undertook a comprehensive study of the types of aircraft most suited to the airline's future requirements. These would involve long-range jets for expansion into the international field, and short-haul jets for growing internal services. Although the Vickers Super VC-10 and BAC One-Eleven were considered, the management advised in favour of the Boeing 707-320B and 737. However, when the Board met in August 1966 to consider this recommendation, it failed to reach agreement and the re-equipment decision was postponed. It was during this period that the airline was subjected to considerable political influences which were to have significant results in the future. One such force was the desire of the Singapore Government to see its equal partnership status reflected in the name of the joint airline. This was finally achieved in December 1966 when representatives of the two Governments agreed that, from January 1 1967, Malaysian Airways would be known as Malaysia-Singapore Airlines. The carrier's international network was expanded during 1967 to encompass Perth and Taipei, utilising Comet equipment; whilst a chartered Boeing 707-338 was wet-leased from Qantas to inaugurate the Singapore-Sydney route. The following year saw three of the carrier's own 707s being delivered. Its route network was extended to Tokyo, whilst a sixteen-storey MSA head office was opened. Britten Norman BN-2A Islanders started service in East Malaysia. The first five Boeing 737-100s were delivered in 1969, thus replacing the Comet. Services to Bali were introduced, whilst a further Islander was added to the fleet. The year 1970 not only ushered in the new decade, but also saw the inauguration of routes between Bangkok and Hong Kong, and between Kuala Lumpur/Singapore and Colombo, as well as to Madras. It was announced on January 26 1971 that the Malaysian and Singapore Governments had agreed to set up separate national airlines, following differences of views and opinions. April 1 that year saw thrice-weekly flights to Melbourne begin and, by June, flights to Bombay, Bahrain, Rome and London (LHR) were added to its network. That same year saw increased frequencies to Australia and Jakarta, as well as a decision by the airline to convert all of its five Boeing 707s to have the Superjet interior. Another new port of call was added to the ever-increasing network. This time, in February 1972, it was Saigon, which had thrice weekly services. An increase in frequency was also made to Jakarta. In June of that year, the first step in the abandonment of MSA was when Singapore created its own airline, Singapore Airlines. August 1 saw the introduction of four more new destinations, with services to Athens and Zurich twice weekly, Frankfurt and Osaka thrice weekly. Flights to the UK were increased to five per week. October 1 1972 was a sad day in aviation history, since the company known as Malaysia-Singapore Airlines ceased to exist. From that time onwards both Singapore and Malaysia had their own carriers. Depicted here at Perth, in April 1971, is one of the five Boeing 707s operated by MSA. This night time shot captures, rather well, the colourful livery of this Far Eastern airline. *(B. J. Eagles)*

MIDDLE EAST AIRLINES (ME/MEA)   Lebanon

The national airline of the worn-torn state of Lebanon, was formed in May 1945 by Lebanese businessmen, and commenced de Havilland Rapide services between Beirut and Nicosia on November 20 of that year; the line was subsequently expanded to Baghdad. Continental European services began with Viscount aircraft, along a Beirut–Athens–Rome route in November 1955. Since then, the company has greatly expanded its scheduled passenger network, assisted by a merger with Air Liban in November 1965, and the acquisition of Lebanese International Airlines' traffic rights in 1969. In 1985, MEA once again re-established its international services following Lebanese civil strife. A shutdown of Beirut International Airport, forced the airline to suspend scheduled operations between February 6 and June 9 1984. The company is presently owned by Inta Investments (62.5 per cent), and Air France (28.5 per cent), and during its troubled times has been based at Paris. Currently, MEA maintains a scheduled network of services to points in Europe, Africa, the Middle East and New York (JFK), in the USA. The airline uses an ageing fleet of Boeing 707s and 720s. Three Boeing 747s that were leased-out to other airlines during the raging war, have since been returned and are utilised on the airlines' network. A quantity of Airbus A310 types have recently been introduced, to allow a fleet renewal, during the current cease-fire in the Lebanon. Inspiration for the MEA livery was obtained from the national flag, with the Lebanese 'Cedar Tree' appearing within a white disk on the all-red fin. An orthodox red windowline is trimmed either side by a red pinstripe, separating the white cabin roof from the natural-metal lower fuselage and simple 'MEA' lettering in red is worn near the forward passenger door. It should be noted that the registration appears in white on the tail and full-length 'Middle East Airlines Air Liban' titles are carried on the rear part of the cheatline. The Boeing 747s, at the time of writing however, sport a different livery. An all-white fuselage is punctuated with red 'MEA' titles on the forward fuselage. The registration appears in black, at the rear. The carrier's ICAO call sign is 'CEDAR JET'.

MILLION AIR (OX/OXO)   United States of America

Million Air, named after its founder, J. B. Million, was established in 1983 and commenced freight charter services out of Miami, Florida in July of the following year. An initial fleet of two Canadair CL-44-D4, purchased from the Westinghouse Corporation in 1984, and a sole Douglas DC-7CF, all in freighter configuration, were maintained. Today, a single Boeing 707-320C, N722GS, is operated and, as a Miami based carrier, it operates scheduled and charter freight services within the USA and to South America. The first livery sported by Million Air comprised of two narrow pinstripes in green and black, which flowed over a base metal fuselage finish, and accommodated simple black 'Million Air' titles. The tail fin displayed a huge Dollar sign in green, which hinted that the titles should perhaps have been read as 'Millionaire'! It should be noted that the owner's 'JBM' initials in blue were positioned alongside the crew door, whilst a small black 'cargo' inscription was situated on the tail. Nowadays the Boeing 707 sports a livery not dissimilar to

what it used to be. The aircraft is painted in an overall white finish. The Dollar tail logo still dominates the vertical fin, whilst black 'Million Air' titles are situated on the forward fuselage. A thick-set cheatline runs the entire length of the fuselage, whilst miniature bands run above and below this line. The registration, in black letters, is positioned behind the rear door. 'Gulf Sierra' made its first flight on December 4 1967, and was delivered to Pan American World Airways, as N463PA, a week later. 'Clipper Queen of the East' had construction number 19373. In October 1975, ATASCO Leasing purchased the aircraft, before it was sold to Air France, a month later, as F-BYCO. The French carrier made good use of the 707 before eventually disposing of it to Pan Aviation, in June 1983, as N722GS. It was not until January 25 1988 that Million Air leased the aircraft, with whom it is currently in service. The carrier's ICAO call sign is 'MILLAIR'. *(Author's Collection)*

MISR OVERSEAS AIRWAYS (MO)   Egypt

Misr Overseas Airways, an Egyptian carrier, provides scheduled and charter services from its Cairo base. The airline operates scheduled cargo flights to Koln, Khartoum and Maribor (Yugoslavia). The company was formerly known as Air Lease Egypt, and adopted its present name in October 1983, when it commenced its own operations. Passenger and cargo charters are maintained to Africa, Asia, Europe and Latin America. A fleet of Boeing 707 aircraft is operated. The airline livery consists of a conventional cheatline arrangement in red and turquoise that underlines full length 'Misr Overseas Airways' titling, which appears in a unique character style

designed to convey a sense of Egypt's rich heritage, and is separated from its Arabic translation by the Egyptian flag. The tail fin displays an ingenious motif of the initials 'MOA', arranged in the form of a red sun rising from behind turquoise mountains. This livery is worn by some of the Boeing 707s operated, but not all, as seen by the 707 depicted here. This aircraft is seen sporting a livery reminiscent of Air India, but is in fat the result of a colour scheme once worn by Global International Airways. Additional 'MISR Overseas' titles in black, in both English and Arabic script, have been added. *(K. G. Wright)*

OLYMPIC AIRWAYS (OA/OAL)   Greece

Olympic Airways was founded in 1957 when Aristotle Onassis took over TAE — Greek National Airlines (founded in 1951 through a merger of TAE, Hellas and Aero Metafoa Ellados) which had been nationalised in 1954. Onassis' 50 year concession gave him sole designation to operate a national airline and a monopoly on domestic routes. Onassis withdrew in 1974 following heavy losses, and the airline was grounded pending reorganisation. Settlement was reached in August 1975, and operations were resumed in January 1976. Today the national airline of Greece is wholly Government-owned. Scheduled passenger and cargo services are operated to 31 cities and islands in Greece, and 39 desinations throughout Europe, Africa, the Near, Middle and Far East, Asia, Australia, Canada and the USA. An Athens-Bangkok-Tokyo (NRT) route started in April. Subsidiaries include Olympic Aviation, a company formed in 1971, which operates light aircraft and helicopters on charter, air taxi and flying-training duties. Other subsidiaries include Olympic catering and Olympic Air Tours. A fleet of Boeing 707, 727, 737, 747 and Airbus A300 types is operated. Prior to the present Government, Olympic had outstanding an order for three Boeing 767s. However, following the change in power, the order was subsequently cancelled, and in its place an order for several Boeing 737-400 types was made. The carrier's current livery was introduced in mid 1960 on their first jet equipment — the de Havilland Comet 4. Previously the Douglas DC-3, DC-4 and DC-6 piston engined equipment was operated in a similar livery, but without the multi-coloured Olympic circles in the vertical position on the fin. Instead the motif consisted of five small white circles on a bar and cross bar insignia. In 1960 the Olympic flag in its rectangular form preceded the main fuselage logo, but by the mid sixties this flag was modified into its present 'waving' streamlined form. Most of Olympic's present fleet bear individual aircraft names. Seen here at Frankfurt Airport, in May 1987, is Boeing 707-384B, SX-DBE. The Greek national flag carrier's ICAO call sign is 'OLYMPIC'. *(W. Kathe)*

PAN AMERICAN WORLD AIRWAYS (PA/PAA)

United States of America

Pan Am was originally formed in March 1927 to operate a United States Postal Service contract between Key West in Florida and Havana in Cuba. Considerable international route expansion took place in the post-war years, so that by the mid-1960s the carrier had an extensive worldwide network of services. During 1979 the Metropolitan Air Facilities division (general aviation services), the Aerospace Services division (support for Kennedy Space Centre missile activities), and the Airline Services division (airline and airport technical and management assistance) were merged into Pan Am World Services, with headquarters at the striking Pan Am Building in New York City. The airline then became the second largest carrier in the USA in 1979, by acquiring a majority stock-holding in National Airlines of Miami. Full integration of the two companies was implemented following the 1980 summer season. In February 1986 Pan Am sold its entire Pacific division to United Airlines, and on April 17 of that year it acquired Ransome Airlines. This airline subsequently began services in the following June as 'Pan Am Express', feeding mainly Pan Am's New York (JFK) hub. Today an extensive network of scheduled passenger services exists, covering over fifty-six destinations in the USA, fourteen in the Caribbean, ten in South America, plus Europe, the Middle East and Asia. The carrier is the largest operating at New York (JFK). Following the loss of its Pacific division, Pan Am concentrated on expanding its transatlantic services. Nine new European destinations (Leningrad, Moscow (SVT), Milan, Oslo, Helsinki, Stockholm, Prague, Krakow and Shannon) were added in 1986. A network of local services in Germany is also maintained. In December of that year Pan Am became the first US carrier to link the USA and Saudi Arabia directly, with a same aircraft New York (JFK)-Frankfurt-Riyadh service. At the end of 1990, the airline started the process of selling most of its transatlantic services to United Airlines, and as of April 4, completely ceased all services to/from the UK. The current livery was proposed by Airbus Industrie to coincide with the delivery of the first A300s, and has now been adopted fleetwide. Regarded as one of the most effective liveries of today, the new image employs a plain white fuselage down to wing level, with huge 'PAN AM' titles in blue. The historic globe logo on the tail, encompasses the entire fin. A fleet of Boeing 727, 737, 747, Airbus Industrie A300 and A310 aircraft is maintained. The carrier's ICAO call sign is 'CLIPPER'. Seen here on approach to London's Heathrow, is Boeing 707-321, N732PA. The aircraft, 'Clipper Mercury', was on the final stages of its non-stop flight from New York's (JFK). *(B. J. Eagles)*

PORTS OF CALL AIRLINES (PC/SPC)

United States of America

Ports Of Call Airlines was formed in April 1966 as the Ports of Call Travel Club, with a single Douglas DC-7, and over the next twenty years became the United States' largest and most successful club of its type. A change of name to Skyworld was made in 1985, followed a couple of years later by the name it finally adopted. Unfortunately, entry into the nineties did little for Ports Of Call, and due to various problems it was forced to shut down its entire operations. Its fleet of Boeing 707 aircraft have been put into storage. Prior to the company's demise it offered extensive domestic and international jet charters from its base at Denver, Colorado. It should be noted that the passengers who flew with the carrier were treated like VIPs, right from the commencement of their journey. Ports Of Call was fortunate to have its own exclusive terminal, baggage handling, customs and catering department, which enabled the carrier to operate independently from the rest of the Denver Stapleton Airport. The various name changes that occurred throughout Ports Of Call's existence had little effect on its livery, with only the replacement of the previous name by the new one, in bright red. The remainder of the original scheme, including the narrow yellow cheatline running over a blue lower fuselage and deep blue undersides, as well as the yellow globe fin motif with an 'S' (when the Skyworld name was used) were retained. It should be noted that all fleet members carried the last three digits of their registrations as a fleet number, in yellow on the lower forward fuselage. Depicted here is one of the company's Boeing 707 aircraft. The photograph, taken in March 1987, portrays the livery of the airline when it was still using the name Skyworld. *(K. G. Wright)*

QANTAS AIRWAYS (QF/QFA)   Australia

The oldest airline in the English-speaking world, Qantas was originally formed to operate Australian outback flights within Queensland in November 1920, by two young Australian aviators (Hudson Fysh and Paul McGinness). The acronym, QANTAS, stands for Queensland and Northern Territorial Aerial Services. Regular flights were begun in November 1922 over a Charleville–Cloncurry line. International services to Singapore commenced in 1934 and by 1947, Qantas was flying to London. There followed a period of rapid expansion and today the nation's flag carrier flies on a scheduled basis to points throughout the world, connecting Australia with Europe, the Middle East, Africa, Asia and North America. The fleet was, until the eighties, an all-Boeing 747 affair, with some twenty-six of the type in several variants, series 200s, 300s

and SPs, but in July 1985, the first of a number of Boeing 767-200ERs was delivered, for use on some regional services, for they are better suited. These were later joined by the series 300, operated on some of the lower density Far Eastern flights. The superb current livery, a creation of the Lunn Design Group of Sydney, was officially unveiled in June 1985. A 'dynamic and proudly Australian' image is conjured by the sleek white kangaroo which is contained within an all-red tail fin, continuing around the lower part of the tail fin and trimmed in gold at the leading edge for added elegance and sophistication. The remainder of the fuselage is pure white, promoting 'Qantas' lettering in black near the forward passenger door. It should be noted that the tail design is repeated on the engines, which are white on the 767s and natural metal on the 747s.

RACE AVIATION
United States of America

RACE Aviation, or giving it its full title, Rent Aviation Cost Efficient, is a pure-freight operator. The company, based in Burbank, California, operates a sole Boeing 707-331C on worldwide charters. Its cargo is diverse, and RACE will carry items from day-old chicks to vehicles. N345FA made its original flight on June 30 1969, before being delivered to its first customer, Trans World Airlines, as N15713 on July 16 of that year. The aircraft then flew many millions of miles with the American carrier, as fleet number '5713', until 1978 when Global International Airlines leased the 707 from July 31; which it subsequently purchased a month later. The aircraft was then named 'Cricket 1' on August 22. Another long period of time followed, and the aircraft finally came into the hands of RACE Aviation in March 1985. However, it kept its previous registration for

a further four months, until July of that year, when it was given the number N345FA. Having spent its life in various colour schemes, it was rather a come down to find that RACE had no intention of repainting the aircraft in its livery. Instead, 'Foxtrot Alpha' was put back to bare metal, with only the company title, RACE, appearing on the upper fuselage. Farhad Azima purchased the 707 in October of that year, but subsequently leased back the aircraft to RACE for a period of twenty months, before it was handed back. Boeing 707-331C, c/n 20069, then made another journey, this time to its new owners, Fast Air of Chile, as CC-CUE, where the aircraft has been on lease since June 1988. Depicted here at Frankfurt is N345FA, in October 1986, having made a long haul flight from the USA.
(B. T. Richards)

ROYAL AIR MAROC (AT/RAM)   Morocco

Royal Air Maroc was formed in June 1953 as Compagnie Cherifienne de Transports Aeriens. The carrier had been brought about through the merger of Societe Air Atlas and Air Maroc; the present title was adopted in 1957, to coincide with the country's independence. Stockholders in the company are the Moroccan Government (with 92.7 per cent), Air France, Compagnie Generale Transatlantique and Aviaco. Today, the Moroccan flag carrier maintains scheduled services from the capital, Casablanca, and also Tangier, to domestic points as well as to destinations in Europe, the Middle East, North and South America. Charter and inclusive tour flights are also undertaken. Subsidiary companies are SOTORAM (Societe Touristique de Royal Air Maroc), which provides catering services and runs three hotels, and Royal Air Inter, which operates domestic flights. Royal Air Maroc's fleet consists of Boeing 707, 727, 737, 747,

757 and ATR-42 types. An order for up to ten Boeing 737-400 and 500 aircraft will be delivered during the nineties, so as to replace the older Series 200s currently in the fleet. Royal Air Maroc's livery has a centrepiece which is displayed in green on the tail as a shooting star, taken from the national flag. The star's bright red tail encircles bold 'RAM' lettering. Lower case 'Royal Air Maroc' titles, again in red, adorn the upper forward fuselage; in English on the starboard and Arabic on the port. Below that is a decorative green and red windowline which has been allowed to taper at both ends. Undersides are left a natural metal on the Boeing 707s, 747s and 757s, whilst a grey paint is applied to the ATR-42s, Boeing 727s and 737s. Depicted here is one of the carrier's Boeing 707s, at Paris. The airline's ICAO call sign is 'MAROCAIR'. *(K. G. Wright)*

SABENA — BELGIAN WORLD AIRLINES (SN/SAB)

Belgium

The Belgian national airline was formed nearly seventy years ago on May 23 1923, to succeed SNETA (which was formed in 1919 and made its first flight in March 1920), which had operated route proving flights within Africa for three years. Sabena began revenue flight activities over a Brussels–Strasbourg route on April 1 1924. Besides its early European operations, the airline was a pioneer in establishing many African services, flying to the Congo, beginning in 1925. Between May 1940 and October 1945, European services were suspended, but African operations continued throughout World War II. Following the restoration of European flights, Sabena began scheduled Atlantic operations between Belgium and the United States, in 1947. Comprehensive scheduled services are now flown throughout Europe and to cities in North America, the Middle East, Asia and Africa. Sabena's sophisticated all-jet fleet employs Boeing 737-200s and -300s for most European routes, and Boeing 747s, Douglas DC-10s and Airbus A310s for extra capacity services and long haul flights. When the Belgian carrier introduced its first A310 in March 1984, a brand new colour scheme was unveiled which has since been adopted fleetwide. A new, lighter blue, cheatline extends along the fuselage length, trimmed either side by narrow pinstripes in the same colour. Matching Sabena titles are displayed on the upper fuselage in a new style, but are still followed by the flag and 'Belgian World Airlines' sub titles. The tail fin design remains unaltered, as it has for many years, this reflecting a traditional stability, with the 'S' disecting a large white disk. The lower fuselage is painted grey in all cases.

SAUDIA — SAUDI ARABIAN AIRLINES (SV/SVA)

Saudi Arabia

Saudia, the national airline of the Kingdom of Saudi Arabia, was formed in 1945 and initially operated a fleet of three Douglas DC-3s. At the same time the airline signed an agreement with TWA for the provision of technical and management assistance. Scheduled passenger and freight services now connect the three main Saudi cities, Jeddah, Riyadh and Dhahran, with over sixty points in Europe, North America, Africa, Asia and the Middle East, as well as linking over twenty domestic communities. It now ranks as the largest airline in the Arab world. A modern, all-jet fleet of Boeing 737, 747, L-1011 TriStar and Airbus A300-600 types is maintained. Several Boeing 707s can be seen in a variation of the Saudia livery, however, these are operated on behalf of the Saudi Royal Family. It should be noted that numerous other aircraft types appear in this livery, but they too are operated for the Royal Family/Government use. The airlines' colour scheme has, essentially, remained unchanged for many years. It still appears both modern and stylish, featuring a double sub-divided cheatline arrangement in two values of green, above two values of blue; these colours being separated by a narrow strip of white. The white upper fuselage contrasts with the polished natural metal undersides and displays a complicated title arrangement, in both English and Arabic, with 'Saudia' in one language and the secondary 'Saudi Arabian Airlines' titles in the other. This sequence is reversed on the opposite side. An all-green fin carries the traditional Saudia logo, which consists of two swords crossed before a palm tree on a white inverted triangle, above small 'Saudia' lettering in English on the starboard side, and Arabic on the port. Operations into London Heathrow commenced on May 1 1967, with Boeing 720Bs. The airlines' ICAO call sign is 'SAUDIA'.

SCIBE AIRLIFT CARGO (ZM)   Zaire

Based at the capital Kinshasa, Scibe Airlift Zaire, the country's largest carrier, offers passenger and cargo charter services to over thirty domestic points throughout Africa, and in the Middle East and Europe, together with worldwide contract charters. A regular trans-Zaire passenger service links Kinshasa in the East with Goma in the West. Scibe was formed in 1979 and is owned by Citizen Bemba Saolona. The Scibe fleet has expanded significantly in recent years, and today the airline maintains an entourage of Boeing 707, 727, Boeing/de Havilland Canada DHC-6 Twin Otter, L-100 Hercules and Fokker F-27 types. The company livery features a rather clever 'SBZ' motif on an otherwise all white fin, and a broad red cheatline which runs along the entire fuselage length, sweeping under the black radar nose at the front. Black 'Scibe-Zaire' titling and the national flag appear below the cheatline on the Friendships, but the

707, 727 and Hercules titles read 'Scibe-Airlift', and are displayed on the cabin roof. Depicted here at Ostend Airport, Belgium, having recently flown in from Kinshasa, is one of the company's two Boeing 707s, 9Q-CBS. The aircraft originally flew on October 11 1969, and was delivered to Sabena the following month as OO-SJO. It stayed with the company until 1980, when it was leased to Zaire International Cargo, but was returned to the Belgian carrier a short while later. The aircraft saw service with Sobelair, and again with Sabena, before being sold to Scibe Airlift Zaire, as 9Q-CBS in January 1985. It was subsequently re-registered 9Q-CBW, following a lease to Naganagani, in June 1987. The aircraft made a short term lease to Air Lanka in 1988, but has subsequently been returned to its owner. *(K. G. Wright)*

SEA GREEN AIR TRANSPORT (ES/ESA)

Antigua

Sea Green Air Transport has operated cargo charter services in the Caribbean area since 1964. Following a period of inactivity, the company was restructured in 1987 and operates passenger and cargo charter using a Boeing/De Havilland Canada DHC-6 Twin Otter, and a Douglas DC-3, from its Antigua base. Worldwide cargo charters are operated from Sea Green's Ostend, Belgium, base. Frequent services to Caracas, Barbados, Martinique, Guadeloupe and Mexico are undertaken. During the 1990 season holiday passenger charters started to use a Convair 990 type. Depicted here at St John's Airport, Antigua, is the carrier's sole Boeing 707-336C, N14AZ. The aircraft originally made its first flight on November 8 1987, and it was delivered to British Overseas Airways Corporation as G-ATWV during the same month. The aircraft

remained with the carrier in 1974, when it merged with British European Airways to form British Airways. As part of a re-equipment programme, the UK airline sold the aircraft, and the Boeing 707 was delivered to Clipper International in January 1982. From there it was leased to West African Cargo as 9G-ACX in February of that year. The aircraft remained with the African airline for a period of four years before being returned to its owner, who subsequently sold the aircraft to Aviation Consultants, as N14AZ. The 707 then saw service with St Lucia Airways, Caribbean Air Transport, and Grecoair, before finally being leased to Sea Green Air Transport. N14AZ has the construction number, 19498.

(K. G. Wright)

SINGAPORE AIRLINES (SQ/SIA)

Singapore

Singapore Airlines was formed on January 28 1972 as the wholly Government-owned national airline of Singapore, to succeed the jointly operated Malaysia-Singapore Airlines. Operations began on October 1 of that year. In November 1985 some sixteen per cent of SIA's expanded stock was sold to local and international investors. This reduced the Government's holding to seventy-three per cent, with a further subsequent reduction to fifty-five per cent in June 1987. The carrier's first two Boeing 747-400 aircraft, dubbed 'MEGATOPS', were delivered in December 1988, and began non-stop Singapore to London (LHR) services in early 1989. SIA's first 747 pure freighter entered service in August of that year, operating to Europe, the Far East and the south-west Pacific. Subsidiary companies include Tradewinds, Singapore Airport Terminal Services, Singapore Engine Overhaul Centre, Singapore Aviation and General Insurance, Singapore International Software Services, Aeroformation Asia and Singapore Properties. Scheduled passenger and cargo services are operated from Singapore to Auckland, Adelaide, Christchurch, Darwin, Port Moresby, Brisbane, Sydney, Melbourne, Perth, Honolulu, Los Angeles, San Francisco, Tokyo (NRT), Osaka, Seoul, Taipei (CKS), Hong Kong, Manila, Bandar Seri Begawan, Jakarta, Fukuoka, Medan, Kuala Lumpur, Kuantan, Penang, Bangkok, Colombo, Cairo, Calcutta, Kathmandu, Denpasar, Delhi, Dhaka, Male, Manchester, Beijing, Shanghai, Karachi, Madras, Bombay, Mauritius, Dubai, Dhahran, Bahrain, Athens, Rome, Vienna, Istanbul, Zurich, Frankfurt, Paris (CDG), Amsterdam, Copenhagen, Brussels and London (LHR). A fleet of Boeing 747 and Airbus A310 aircraft is maintained. On January 16 1990, the company placed a considerable order for the McDonnell Douglas MD 11, which will commence deliveries from the mid-1990s. Depicted here is Boeing 707-312B, 9V-BFB. The aircraft, seen on May 25 1975, is seen at the start of its take-off roll, bound for Singapore. The carrier's ICAO call sign is 'SINGAPORE'. (B. J. Eagles)

SOUTH AFRICAN AIRWAYS (SA/SAA)

South Africa

South African Airways was originally formed in February 1934 to take-over the assets of Union Airways and to operate as a division of South African Railways. The new airline began operations on February 1 1934, with a fleet of single-engine Junkers F13s, later supplemented by a considerable number of Ju52/3Ms and Ju86s. A year later, SAA took over the Junkers-sponsored South-West African Airways, adding Windhoek to its route system. Today the company's scheduled route system includes points in Europe, the Middle and Far East, in addition to regional services within Africa and an extensive domestic network. A mixed fleet of Boeing 737, 747, Airbus A300 and A320 aircraft is maintained. The South African Airways livery is truly bilingual throughout, with titling on the port side in English, and the starboard in Afrikaans, even down to the company logo which reads 'SAA' on one side and the Afrikaans

equivalent 'SAL' on the other. The distinctive bright orange tail fin displays a leaping winged springbok in blue, outlined in white, and a dark blue straight through windowline runs parallel with a narrower line in bright orange below. Highly-polished undersides are a stylish finishing touch, although they are painted grey on the Airbuses. Due to the political differences in South Africa, the airline is unable to fly over Africa to Europe. Thus, flights have to go over the sea, and some route via Sal, Cape Verde Islands. This extra mileage adds considerable flight time to the journey, and thus gives SAA a big disadvantage. It is hoped however, that the political situation will change and thus the African countries involved in the SAA boycott will be more co-operative towards the situation.

SUDAN AIRWAYS (SD/SUD)   Sudan

Sudan Airways was incorporated in 1946 following the signing of an agreement with the British company Airwork Ltd for technical and management assistance. Proving flights were started in April 1947 and regular services followed three months later from Khartoum to Port Sudan, Asmara (Ethiopia) and Juba, using four de Havilland Doves. Today, the state-owned company operates a domestic network extending throughout the Sudan, from Dongola in the north to Juba in the south, and from Geneina in the west to Port Sudan in the east. International routes serve Kano, Nairobi, Addis Ababa, Jeddah, Cario, Abu Dhabi, Doha, Damascus, Baghdad, Tripoli, N'Djamena, Riyadh, Sharjah, Kuwait, Sana'a and with London (LHR), over the 'Blue Nile' route, via Athens, Rome and Frankfurt. This latter line was inaugurated on June 8 1959 with Vickers Viscounts. Charter and survey flights are also undertaken. A fleet of Boeing 707, 737, Fokker F-27 and Fokker F-50 aircraft is maintained. The company has never owned its own wide bodied planes, despite having an order for Airbus types in the mid eighties. However, in saying this, it did lease-in a Lockheed L-1011 Tristar Series 500, JY-AGH, from Royal Jordanian Airlines over the period from March 31 1987 to January 14 1988. It was hoped that the airline might purchase an aircraft of this size, but this was not to be. During the lease, the L-1011 flag ship was adorned in the full Sudan Airways livery, which looked very smart on the aircraft. The carrier's colour scheme was introduced on the airline's Boeing 707 aircraft in July 1974. An obvious colour choice of sand yellow and Nile blue is very originally styled in an elongated 'S' for Sudan, to sweep along the fuselage and culminate in black 'Sudan' titling sweeping along the leading edge of the fin. No fuselage logo is carried and the Sudan fin titling is in English on both the port and starboard surfaces. The name 'Blue Nile' appears on the aft fuselage on one Boeing 707 and one Boeing 737, whilst the name 'White Nile' adorns another 707 and 737 on their rear fuselages. The Sudanese flag appears on the aircraft's upper forward fuselage. The Sudan Airways bird motif is still carried, but in very small size on the yellow cheatline, just below the flight deck windows; although in August 1976 one of the Boeing 707s was seen to be wearing an enlargement of this motif on the forward fuselage, ahead of the wing leading edge. Depicted here, on approach to London Heathrow on August 16 1973, is Boeing 707-321, G-AYBJ. The aircraft was at the time on lease from British Midland Airways. The carrier's ICAO call sign is 'SUDANAIR'. *(B. J. Eagles)*

TAAG — ANGOLA AIRLINES (DT/DTA)

Angola

TAAG, the national flag carrier of the State of Angola, in Southern Africa, was originally formed as DTA Angola Airlines in September 1938 as a division of the Administration of Railways, Harbours and Air Transport Authority of Portuguese West Africa. The carrier ceased being a subsidiary on October 1 1973, and adopted its present title, TAAG Angola Airlines, following Angola's independence in 1975. Linhas Aereas de Angola operates an extensive network of scheduled passenger and cargo services from its base at Luanda to over twenty domestic points in Angola, plus international routes to Sao Tome, Kinshasa, Sal, Brazzaville, Maputo, Lusaka, Havana, Paris (CDG), Rome, Berlin-Schonefeld, Lisbon, Moscow (SVT), Ostend and Rio de Janeiro. The airline has two associated companies, TAAG-Air Charter (with a fleet of two Boeing 707-320C operating cargo flights) and TAAG-Aviacao Ligeira (general aviation). A fleet of Boeing 707, 737, L-100 Hercules, Fokker F-27 and Yakovlev Yak-40 aircraft is maintained together with an L-1011 Tristar SIS 500 on lease from Air Portugal. An extremely bright and modern livery adorns all aircraft of the fleet, based on twin cheatlines in red and orange, which commence under the 'chin' and sweep along the fuselage, with the upper red line finally encompassing the tail. The traditional 'TAAG' lettering has, in recent years, given way to a more internationally recognisable 'Angola Airlines' titling, which appears in black letters on the cabin roof alongside the national flag. The centrepiece of the scheme, however, must be that of the striking tail motif, which is essentially a black 'Antelope head' within an orange disk, formed by its long curved horns. Seen here at Berlin SXF on April 17 1989 is Boeing 707-349C, D2-TOJ of TAAG, sporting the airline's outstanding colour scheme. The carrier's ICAO call sign is 'ANGOLA'. *(K. G. Wright)*

TRANSAVIA AIRLINES (HV/TRH)   Netherlands

Transavia was formed in 1965 to operate inclusive tour charters from its base at Amsterdam's Schipol Airport, using a fleet of piston-engined Douglas DC-6B aircraft. Charter and inclusive-tour operations began on November 17 1966, when the Dutch Dancing Theatre was flown to Naples, Italy. In 1967, the airline changed its name to Transavia Holland, having been known as Transavia (Limburg) NV. The first jet to be operated by the airline, arrived during the same year, in the shape of a Boeing 707. Sud Est 210 Caravelle jets were added in 1969, with Boeing 737s arriving in 1974. The current title was adopted in the eighties, to allow for a more modern image, and at the same time a new livery was adopted. The company is now an all-jet airline flying Dutch holiday-makers to traditional destinations throughout Europe and to North Africa, and in addition is involved heavily in leasing aircraft to other carriers. The current fleet comprises of Boeing 737 (-200 and -300), and 757 types. Although the livery is now different to that shown, the Boeing depicted here sports an extremely innovative scheme for its time. For its centrepiece is a large black 'T' logo, under the cockpit windows. This generates two green fuselage lines, light green from the horizontal stroke and dark green from the vertical, in an overall speeding 'T' effect. The black logo is repeated on the tail, outlined in white, and simple black 'Transavia Holland' lettering adorns the upper white fuselage. Although the majority of the company's fleet did, at one time, wear this livery, the leasing business, operated by Transavia, did lead to a number of hybrid colours with 'Transavia Holland' titles. A large part of the airlines' revenue is derived from worldwide leasing. In February 1986, Transavia introduced a new colour scheme, which has now been applied fleetwide. The familiar two-tone green cheatline emanating from a 'T' motif near the cockpit windows, has been replaced by dark green stripes, separated by lines of light green, red and orange. The initial 'T' still heads the cheatline, but now in green outline, with the horizontal stroke continuing along the cabin. An all white fin displays new-style 'Transavia' titles in green, apart from the black letter 'T', leaving the cabin roof clear apart from the Dutch flag alongside the main passenger door. Transavia is now an associate of KLM — Royal Dutch Airlines.

TRANSBRASIL (TR/TBA)   Brazil

Transbrasil was formed in Sao Paulo on January 5 1955 as Sadia Airlines to carry fresh meat from Concordia to Sao Paulo for the Sadia Organisation, utilising a single Douglas DC-3. Regular services between Sao Paulo, Joacaba, Videira and Florianopolis were inaugurated in March 1956, and the airline proceeded to develop routes in Brazil's south-east. Transportes Aereos Salvador was absorbed in 1962, thereby expanding links into the north-eastern part of the country. In 1972 the carrier transferred its headquarters to Brazilia and was renamed Transbrasil. In June 1976 the company joined with the Government of Bahia state to establish the regional Nordeste airline, which subsequently took over various local routes, allowing Transbrasil to concentrate on mainline traffic development. During the 1950s and 1960s Sadia utilised Douglas DC-3 and Curtiss Commando C-46 piston aircraft. In the mid-1960s Handley Page Herald turboprops were acquired, and by the early 1970s BAe 1-11 twinjets were in service. In 1973 Transbrasil added Embraer 110 Bandeirante turboprops, and began adding Boeing 727-100 jets the following year. Boeing 767 jet equipment was added in 1983, and in the same year the carrier acquired used Boeing 707 cargo equipment. Today the airline operates scheduled passenger and cargo services from Brazilia to points in south-east and north-east Brazil, and a cargo service to Miami. The carrier has begun its first international route, a thrice-weekly service from Sao Paulo to Orlando, which is flown by Boeing 767-200s. Transbrasil is owned by the Fontana family. An all-Boeing fleet of 707, 727, 737 and 767 types is operated. During the early eighties the airline had an outstanding order for a total of nine Boeing 757-200s. However, these were subsequently cancelled in 1983. All seven colours of the rainbow appear in stripes on the tail of Transbrasil's aircraft, contrasting with the fuselage which is pure white, apart from the 'Transbrasil' titles and sun motif, a remnant of the company's Sadia days. In a unique twist to the scheme, each aircraft has a theme of one of six tail shades to colour the titles, registration and wing surfaces. It should be noted that Transbrasil freighters carry 'Cargo' titles reversed out in the tail colours in white. The carrier's ICAO call sign is 'TRANSBRASIL'. *(K. G. Wright)*

TRANS MEDITERRANEAN AIRWAYS (TL/TMA)

Lebanon

Trans Mediterranean Airways was formed in 1953 and for six years operated as a non-scheduled airline. Initial operations began using two York freighters on non-scheduled cargo services from Beirut to oil stations in the Arabian Gulf. It became a joint stock company in October 1959, and scheduled all-cargo services began the same year. TMA was wholly owned by its former president, Munir Abu Haidar, between 1959 and November 1986. On February 12 1959 a cabinet decree was obtained whereby TMA was certificated by the Lebanese Government for the carriage of freight on regular scheduled routes; charter activities, however, continued for some years. On April 14 1971, TMA inaugurated the first round-the-world cargo services from Beirut to Karachi, Bombay, Bangkok, Singapore, Manila, Taipei, Osaka, Tokyo, Anchorage, New York (JFK), Amsterdam, Basle and Beirut. The majority shareholder is Jet Holdings. N9676 operated the company's first Boeing 747 all freight flight from New York (JFK) to Beirut, via Amsterdam, on May 16 1975. The aircraft carried the now standard TMA livery of green and yellow, but for initial services retained the American registration letters in white. This aircraft was on wet lease from American Airlines and was joined by a second Boeing 747 during the latter part of 1975. The 747 wearing its new Lebanese registration, OD-AGC, first visited London Heathrow on September 21 1975. Upper and lower wing and tail surfaces were white, with the ailerons and elevators in a natural metal finish. The under fuselage was also left in a natural metal finish. The crew door on the right-hand side of the aircraft's upper fuselage was outlined in yellow. Due to a number of factors, the two 747s were subsequently sold, and have not been replaced. The high-visibility TMA colour scheme features a green overall fuselage finish, to contrast with the sand-coloured scenery of the Middle East, its main sphere of operations. The bright yellow tail displays the company motif of a yellow triangle with superimposed green 'TMA' lettering and black wings, all within a green disk, and is topped by the national flag. The green fuselage is violated only by the registration and 'TMA of Lebanon' titles in yellow, with a small version of the tail motif appearing near the cockpit windows. A large fleet of Boeing 707s is operated. However, the fleet has been reduced in recent years, due to the conflict within the Lebanon. The carrier's ICAO call sign is 'TMA'. *(K. G. Wright)*

TRANSPORTES AEREO RIOPLATENSE (HR/HRT)

Argentina

Transportes Aereo Rioplatense was formed in December 1969 by its president, Carols Martinez Guerreo, and associates. Operations began on March 24 1971 using a single swing-tail CL-44 carrying cattle from Houston to Buenos Aires. July 1978 saw the arrival of the company's first pure-jet equipment, in the shape of an ex-Dan Air Boeing 707-321C. Today the carrier, a privately-owned Argentine freight airline, operates regular but unscheduled jet flights in the Western Hemisphere, and offers worldwide charter and contract services in addition to its numerous internal network. TAR now combines operations with Aerotransportes Entre Rios (AER Airlines). Services link Buenos Aires with Bolivia (Santa Cruz), Brazil (Porto Alegre, Rio de Janeiro and Sao Paulo), Chile (Santiago), Paraguay (Asuncion), Uruguay (Montevideo) and the United States (Miami, New York (JFK) and Houston). Flights also operated to Europe, with

the United Kingdom and Italy, being the main two destinations. However, a fortnightly Buenos Aires-Basle service was opened in 1976. The company livery is essentially a simple overpaint of the blue and gold British Caledonian cheatlines, which are now both deep blue, accommodating a huge 'TAR' logo with somewhat exaggerated tails on the letters 'A' and 'R'. It should be noted that identical logos appear on both sides of the aircraft so that the tails point towards the nose on the port side, but towards the rear on the starboard. The fuselage motif is repeated within a white disk in the centre of an otherwise all blue fin, and below a facsimile of the Argentine flag. The word 'Cargo' above the wings describes the nature of TAR's business. Depicted here, in November 1986, is one of the two ex-Dan Air Boeing 707s purchased by TAR. *(K. G. Wright)*

TRANS WORLD AIRLINES (TW/TWA)

United States of America

Trans World Airlines is today, one of the world's largest airlines, offering scheduled passenger services over a vast network, which includes over fifty domestic cities in the USA, and reaches to Europe, the Middle East and Asia, as well as passenger charters. At the time of writing, the airline was trying to sell its transatlantic services into London (LHR), to American Airlines. With the backing of the United States Government, and the UK Transport Secretary, it remains only for the UK Aviation Authorities to 'rubber stamp' the deal. Therefore, by the time this book is read, it would seem unlikely for TWA to be flying many services into the UK. TWA can trace its history back over sixty years, to 1925, when Western Air Express successfully bid for a US postal service mail contract, over the Salt Lake City–Los Angeles route. In July 1930, Western Air Express merged with Transcontinental Air Transport–Maddux Air Lines, and became known as Trans Continental and Western Air

(TWA). Four years after international services were inaugurated in 1946, the present, more appropriate, title was adopted. On November 30 1974, TWA unveiled its new livery to replace the traditional 'twin globe' scheme, which has remained unchanged now for nearly twenty years, apart from the Trans World titling, which now appears in solid red, replacing the previous red outline. Thin warm red cheatlines commence at the nose under the black anti-dazzle panels and proceed along the pure-white fuselage below the windows, widening as they go and ultimately wrapping around the rear fuselage. The fin displays the white 'TWA' logo reversed out of the red centre section which varies in shape from type to type. Note that the US flag appears at the top of the fin on most types, but on those with a 'T'-tail it is featured alongside the registration

TRINIDAD AND TOBAGO (BWIA INTERNATIONAL) AIRWAYS (BW/BWA)

Trinidad

British West Indian Airways (BWIA), fondly known throughout the trade as 'Bee Wee', was formed on January 1 1980, through the merger of BWIA International and Trinidad and Tobago Air Services (TTAS). BWIA was originally founded in 1940 as one of the TACA group of Central American airlines. Control passed to British South American Airways (later merged in BOAC) in 1947, and the British West Indian Airways title was adopted in 1948. In November 1961 the Trinidad Government acquired a 90% holding, followed by the remainder in 1967. BWIA operated international services to North and South America and Europe; whilst TTAS, formed in June 1974 by the Government, operated high-frequency shuttle flights that linked the two islands of Trinidad and Tobago. The Government subsequently merged both carriers to improve efficiency. Today, the flag carrier operates scheduled passenger and cargo services from Piarco Airport, Port of Spain, to Tobago, Georgetown, Paramaribo, Caracas, San Juan (Puerto Rico), Kingston, St Maarten,

Curaçao, Miami, New York (JFK), Toronto, Frankfurt and London (Heathrow). A fleet of Lockheed L-1011 Tristar Series 500, Douglas DC-9-30 and McDonnel Douglas MD-83 aircraft is operated. Since April 5 1974, British West Indian Airways' gleaming white sunjets have carried the distinctive cheatline in gold, white and Caribbean blue to London Heathrow. The national flag of Trinidad is carried each side of the fuselage as part of the logo. The aircraft's fins carry the popular BWIA emblem — the steelband motif — a fitting symbol for the planes that carry the uniqie Caribbean charm and spirit into the skies and to its far flung destinations. This colourful livery was originally introduced in mid 1969, although several small changes have occurred during the last few yers. When the four Boeing 707-351C aircraft were delivered, each was given an individual name and was christened after a particular bird, and each plane sported an illustration of the bird on its forward fuselage. The airline's ICAO call sign is 'BEE WEE'. *(Author's Collection)*

TURK HAVA YOLLARI — THY
TURKISH AIRLINES (TK/THY)

Turkey

THY was formed by the Ministry of National Defense on May 20 1933 as Devlet Hava Yollari (Turkish State Airlines). The present title was adopted in February 1956 when the airline became a corporation. DHY inaugurated a thrice-weekly service in 1933 between the country's two major cities, Istanbul and Ankara, via Ekisenhir, using de Havilland Rapides. The airline initially concentrated on building up a comprehensive domestic network, but international expansion began in 1949 with routes to Nicosia, Athens and Beirut. Today, THY operates scheduled passenger services that connect Ankara, Istanbul, Antalya, Izmir and Adana with eleven other domestic points. In addition, an extensive network of international scheduled services is operated to Europe, the Middle and Far East, North Africa and the USA. Charter flights are also undertaken to the Black Sea Coast and Mediterranean countries. However, special charters to West Germany (Hamburg, Hanover, Bremen, Stuttgart, Cologne and Dusseldorf) are also maintained for the large number of Turkish contract workers. The airline is owned by the Turkish Government. The current THY livery is composed of the red and white national colours in a stylish pinstripe form. Five narrow red lines form the cheatline, separating the white upper fuselage from the grey undersides, and terminate in a distinctive black anti-dazzle panel at the nose. A band of six broad stripes covers most of the tail fin, interrupted only by a white disk displaying the traditional THY bird logo. An unusually long title arrangement takes up most of the upper fuselage with the black letters reading 'Turk Hava Yollari — Turkish Airlines THY', followed by the national flag, the Turkish version appearing before the English on both sides. Prior to the delivery of the company's first Airbus Industrie A310, it was speculated that the carrier would adopt a new livery. However, this was not the case, and THY opted for the more traditional approach. The airline maintains a fleet of Douglas DC-9, Boeing 727 and Airbus A310 aircraft. The Boeing 707s and Douglas DC-10s once operated by the carrier have now been transferred to BHT (Bogazici Hava Tasimaciligi), a subsidiary formed in December 1986. The Turkish flag carrier's ICAO call sign is 'TURKAIR'. *(K. G. Wright)*

VARIG (RG/VRG)   Brazil

Varig can trace its history back over fifty years to its foundation in May 1927. Its aim was to operate a single Dornier WAL flying boat over the domestic Porto Alegre-Rio Grande route, succeeding the former Kondor Syndikat. The airline subsequently absorbed several other airlines, including the domestic operator Aero Geral (1951), the Real consortium (1961) and Panair do Brazil's equipment and international routes in 1965. Cruzeiro was acquired in 1975. Today, Varig operates an extensive network of routes throughout South and Central America, and to the USA, Europe, Africa and Japan. Domestic operators Cruzeiro and Rio-Sul are subsidiaries. Most of the company's shares are held by the foundation of employees and executives. A fleet of Boeing 707, 727, 737, 747, 767, A300, DC-10 and L-188 Electra aircraft is maintained. Delivery of the first of an order for the McDonnell Douglas MD-11 was made in 1990. The predominant dark blue colour scheme is obtained from the national flag and colours the broad cheatline, which curves round the aircraft's chin and also features a 'seam effect' created by white pinstripes at window level. The famous compass logo is displayed on the fin, above black Varig titling. However, on the fuselage, the company name is repeated in blue alongside the Brazilian flag, and 'Brasil' lettering in black. The overall livery is adapted slightly to fit the shapes of the other aircraft in the fleet. The only really notable exception being the application of the 'flying figurehead' logo positioned above the cheatline on the 747s and most DC-10s and MD-11s in natural metal, the A300s in grey, and some of the DC-10s in a more visually pleasing white. One of the Brazilian flag carrier's Boeing 707s is depicted here whilst on an international flight from Rio de Janeiro, the aircraft having left the airport, some sixty minutes before. The carrier's ICAO call sign is 'VARIG'.

(Varig — Brazilian Airlines)